Honor the Grandmothers

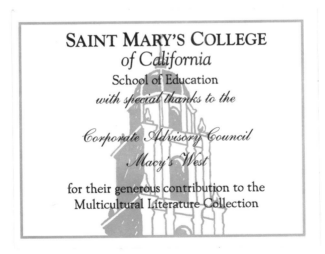

SAINT MARY'S COLLEGE
of California
School of Education
with special thanks to the

Corporate Advisory Council
Macy's West

for their generous contribution to the
Multicultural Literature Collection

COMPILED AND EDITED BY Sarah Penman

Honor the Grandmothers

Dakota and Lakota Women Tell Their Stories

ⵏ MINNESOTA HISTORICAL SOCIETY PRESS

For information, write to the
Minnesota Historical Society Press
345 Kellogg Boulevard West
St. Paul, MN 55102-1906

www.mnhs.org/mhspress

Manufactured in the United States of America

International Standard Book Number
0-87351-384-3 cloth
0-87351-385-1 paper

♾ This paper used in this publication meets the minimum requirements
of the American National Standard for Information Sciences Permanence
for Printed Library materials, ANSI Z39.48-1984

This book has been supported in part by
a grant from the Minnesota Historical Society
with funds provided by the State of Minnesota.

Library of Congress Cataloging-in-Publication Data

Honor the grandmothers: Dakota and Lakota elders tell
their stories/[compiled and edited] by Sarah Penman.
        p. cm.
    ISBN 0-87351-384-3 (cloth: alk. Paper)—ISBN 0-87351-385-1 (pbk.)
    1. Dakota women—Biography.   2. Teton women—Biography.
    3. Dakota aged women—Biography.   4. Teton aged women Biography.
I. Penman, Sarah, 1950–
E99.D1 H75 2000
978'.0049752'00922—dc21
[B]

00-021324

Honor the Grandmothers

Note on Pronunciation

Three vowels are nasalized: the letter "a" as in the word "wander," "i" as in "cinder," and "u" as in "under."

The letter "c" is pronounced like "ch" in "church."

The letter "s" is pronounced like "sh" if the word does not contain a "k" or like "s" if the word does contain a "k."

The letter "z" is pronounced like the "s" in "pleasure."

"H" is a guttural sound.

Introduction

The first time I saw Celane Not Help Him was at the Wounded Knee Cemetery on the Pine Ridge Reservation in southwestern South Dakota. It was December 29, 1989, the ninety-nine-year anniversary of the Wounded Knee Massacre of 1890. A light snow was falling and an arctic wind swept unrelentingly over the pine-dotted buttes.

The Chief Big Foot Memorial Riders, descendants of those who died or were wounded during the massacre, circled the cemetery on horseback. The riders and their supporters had gathered to honor their ancestors with a ceremony of remembrance. Celane Not Help Him, seemingly impervious to the bitter cold, stood solemnly at the gravesite, where the victims of the massacre lay in a mass grave. Just before the ceremony began, I photographed Celane from afar.

It wasn't until the following summer that I saw her again. The Big Foot Riders held a gathering on Stronghold Table in South Dakota's

Badlands, the site of the last ghost dance. Fourteen tipis formed a semi-circle along the ridge, overlooking the Black Hills. An assortment of canvas and dome tents was scattered in the swaying grass; children, dogs, and horses roamed free.

Ron McNeil, a Big Foot rider, came to my camp to peruse the box of photographs I had printed of the previous year's ride. He recognized Celane and offered to take me to her campsite and introduce me. When we arrived, she was busy unpacking food onto a card table. I gave her one of the photographs of herself. She told me that she really doesn't like photographs of herself, but, much to my surprise, she appeared to be moved by the photograph and her eyes became misty. Then she insisted that I sign the back of it. We really didn't talk much then; I simply spent time at her campsite sharing the silence.

A few weeks later I attended the International Brotherhood Pow-wow in the town of Porcupine on the Pine Ridge Reservation. I was strolling through the powwow arbor when I noticed a figure hurrying down the hill toward me. It was Celane Not Help Him; she had been setting up camp when she spotted me. She said she wanted to talk to me, so we drove up to her campsite and sat in the front seat of my car because it had begun to rain. I had been writing articles for *The Circle*, a native newspaper, so I asked her if I could tape-record our conversation, and she agreed.

"Since you were interested in taking pictures and writing the right stories about what happened, I was thinking, when I saw you go by, 'I want to talk to her,' but it's not about little things but back about a hundred years ago, during that time." Then she began to tell me the history of the Wounded Knee Massacre as it had been told to her by her grandfather, Dewey Beard, one of the survivors.

She spoke softly, gazing straight ahead through the rain-spattered windshield, describing the events of the massacre as if she were witnessing them at that moment. I sat, riveted, barely daring to breathe. She spoke for about an hour and ended by simply saying, "That's all I want to tell you."

I was moved by the depth of emotion with which she recounted the history of Wounded Knee, by the horror of the massacre, and by the fact that she had wanted to share it with me. But I had no thought of ever using the interview, and the tape languished on a shelf for many years. I continued traveling throughout South Dakota as time and finances permitted, photographing traditionalist gatherings and writing articles. It is only on reflection that I realize that those moments I spent with Celane Not Help Him marked a turning point in my life; unwittingly, during that conversation, she planted the seeds of what was to become this book.

In traditional Lakota and Dakota society, grandmothers were respected for their knowledge, wisdom, and power as life-givers, healers, dreamers, harvesters, and teachers. Instructing female children in survival skills was the domain of the grandmothers, and they counseled girls on their moral, social, and spiritual responsibilities.

During the lifetimes of today's elders, Lakota and Dakota culture was profoundly affected by U.S. government policies such as the boarding-school system for Indian children and tribal relocation. Today, modern and traditional values as well as rural and urban experiences exist side by side in many native communities. Again it is the grandmothers who shoulder the task of maintaining traditions and retelling the old stories—not simply as memories from the past, but as living elements in the contemporary American Indian experience.

But speaking about the grandmothers and their role in their communities in the third person or in the past tense does not do them justice. They can tell their own stories. That is why this book exists.

In 1991, through a series of serendipitous events, I received a grant from the Minnesota Historical Society to gather the oral traditions of Lakota and Dakota women elders. My primary concern as a wasicun win—white woman—was to portray accurately a community and culture that has frequently been misrepresented.

I was born in Scotland, the second daughter of working-class parents. By all accounts, my destiny was to follow in the footsteps of my ancestors, who were sheepherders and flax-thrashers on one side, furnace-feeders and charwomen on the other. However, at the age of twenty I arrived on the shores of America with all my worldly possessions in one suitcase. I came for three months. I have lingered for twenty-nine years.

My interest in the native community began in 1988 when I was invited to accompany a friend to the Cheyenne River Reservation in central South Dakota. I immediately felt at home. This sense of belonging can be attributed to the generosity and acceptance I have experienced from community members.

Initially, I had no thought of photographing or writing about

American Indians. However, as I came to know people, I began to document issues and events that were of importance to them. I had begun by writing for *The Circle* but as I listened to the stories that people told me, my focus shifted to recording oral histories. The ancient art of oral tradition is a powerful means of expression and I hoped I would be able to share some of the elders' wisdom and knowledge with others.

In July 1991, I set forth, tape recorder in unreliable car, to traverse the highways and byways of South Dakota in search of the "grandmas." Little did I realize that while interpreting another culture's history may be difficult, simply gathering it would prove my first challenge!

Two days after I reached South Dakota, my car, on which I had just spent $500 for repairs, committed hara-kiri over a cliff. For $400, I bought a bright red 1964 Ford Fairlane station wagon which bore an uncanny resemblance to a gaudy hearse. After many delays, and more breakdowns, I set off from Rapid City. The Ford proceeded to break down in various yards all across the Pine Ridge reservation, and I spent a solid month with my head under its gaping hood, wondering why it kept overheating. In Pine Ridge village, I was introduced to two grandmothers who graciously let me pitch my tent in their yard, while the local garage systematically, at a snail's pace, stripped my car of every part but the ailing one.

Panic set in as these women, while an endless source of delightful stories, refused to utter even one sound into my tape recorder, undoubtedly because we had only recently met. Stranded in Pine Ridge village, I had no way of reaching the grandmothers I did know who had been anticipating my arrival. Meanwhile, I performed household tasks in exchange for meals and showers. On more than one occasion, as I labored over my mop bucket, I'd reflect on the glamorous life I was leading as a historian.

Finally, after weeks of trial with no tribulations, my car was deemed roadworthy, and having run out of money, I was forced to go home. I yearned for my own lumpy bed, a warm bath, and the joy of sitting in front of my computer. In Minneapolis, however, I arrived home to discover that my house had been ransacked hours before my arrival and everything of monetary and sentimental value had been stolen. I vowed that my travels in South Dakota had come to a merciful conclusion.

I was beginning to doubt myself. My initial plan had been to gather a few oral histories but I had felt that they would be wasted, languishing in an archive, and I wanted to share them with a wider audience. Monika Bauerlein, a journalist and radio producer, had suggested producing a radio documentary, and I had just received a grant from the Minnesota Humanities Commission in support of this endeavor. Funders were expecting me to deliver the fruits of my labor, but there was no fruit! I was beside myself. Monika, and Juanita Espinosa, a Dakota-Ojibwe radio host and director of the Native Arts Circle, an organization dedicated to promoting the work of native artists, were enlisted to help with the project, and together we began the process of recording elders. Juanita suggested I contact Iola Columbus, who had been the first female tribal chairperson in Minnesota. She had been working to organize a Grandmothers' Society dedicated to passing on the traditional stories and values. We visited her in Morton, Minnesota.

At this point the idea of returning to South Dakota was far from my mind. But slowly I began to yearn for the wide skies and rolling prairies, and I determined to go back.

One cold winter morning in 1992, with more than a little trepidation, Monika, Juanita, and I set off for points west. This trip was not without its hazards, but the grandmothers welcomed us at every turn.

Obstacles to be overcome included the lack of quiet interview locations in homes brimming with occupants, barking dogs, blaring television sets, and the hum of appliances. Working with the elderly also proved more of a problem than anticipated. Several of the women we had hoped to interview became ill, one broke her ankle, and one suffered the loss of her husband, resulting in a long delay before we returned to interview her again. Inclement weather, icy roads, and blizzards also slowed us down.

But some of the obstacles also proved fortuitous. Stranded in Rapid City with spare time on our hands, we landed in the kitchen of Cecilia Montgomery, an elder whose name had been passed on by Juanita's grandmother. Though elders are often said to be reserved toward strangers, Cecilia immediately began talking a mile a minute and did not stop for several hours. "I've always been known for my big mouth," she grinned.

On our return to Minnesota, I contacted Stella Pretty Sounding Flute, whom I had first met in 1988 in Aberdeen, South Dakota, as she prepared food and shelter for participants in the Spiritual Walk for the Sacred Pipe, a 450-mile trek across South Dakota. Monika and I drove to Aberdeen—through another blizzard—and spent a night and a day at Stella's house, almost continuously recording as she spoke of her life and her art as a star-quilt maker.

Two years and several road trips later, the four grandmothers had filled more than forty hours of tape. The duration of the recording sessions varied but generally lasted from three to four hours. Upon returning to Minnesota, the interviews were transcribed, and any points that required clarification were noted for future interviews. In 1993 our one-hour radio documentary, "Honor the Grandmothers," was broadcast nationally via satellite.

Much of the interview material, however, could not be used in the radio documentary because of time constraints. This book seemed the only way to do justice to their stories. But editing their words into book form has also proved to be a lengthy process. Each woman received a complete transcript of all her interviews, as well as the shortened, edited, and occasionally rearranged texts. For example, over the course of recording the grandmothers, they frequently repeated the same stories, often adding new information. These stories were woven together to incorporate as many details as possible. All of the changes were discussed in person, which required several road trips to each of their homes. They were given the opportunity to remove from or add to their words in order to be as accurate as possible. Any errors or omissions are mine. In editing their stories, I have endeavored to retain the flavor of the language as it was spoken. These life histories that the grandmothers and I present reflect ten years of friendship, cooperation, and collaboration.

The women interviewed are Celane Not Help Him, Lakota; Stella

Pretty Sounding Flute, Dakota; Cecilia Montgomery, Lakota; and Iola Columbus, Dakota. In the strong oral tradition of the Lakota-Dakota Nation, cultural continuity is assured through the rituals and practices of the people. The grandmothers' personal stories are living history; during their lifetimes they witnessed what was intended to be the final assault on native land, life, culture, and spirituality. Now elders, they recall their lives as wives, mothers, teachers, keepers of the traditional ways, and role models in their communities. Readers will discover how traditional culture continues to influence modern life, linking past, present, and future.

It has been more than ten years since I first laid eyes on Celane Not Help Him. I still marvel at the fortuitous chain of events that led me to the reservations of South Dakota and Minnesota and to my relationships with the grandmothers.

The last time I saw Celane Not Help Him was at Pine Ridge's Manderson school gymnasium in December of 1997. She had just been released from the hospital and still wore a white, plastic identification bracelet around her wrist. Despite her frailty, she had come to Manderson to honor the Future Generations Riders, the youth that have continued to ride down the Big Foot trail in commemoration of Wounded Knee. She asked her daughter Joyce Not Help Him to assist her in walking to the restroom, and the two of them were halfway across the expanse of gymnasium floor heading for the exit when a drum group began drumming and singing. Celane made a sharp right turn in time to the music and began to dance around, her clenched right fist raised proudly in the air. When the drumming stopped she proceeded on her way. Upon returning to her seat, she explained that the drum group had been singing a Lakota warrior's song. When I teased her about looking like a radical, she said with a grin, "That's me, I'm a radical!"

Celane Not Help Him passed away in December 1998. Iola Columbus is also gone. In 1999, I had the pleasure of seeing Stella Pretty Sounding Flute in Costa Rica. Now in her seventies, she was part of a Lakota Nation delegation celebrating World Peace and Prayer Day, an international gathering of indigenous peoples. Eager to share her knowledge, Stella spoke about her culture and donned her regalia to perform the Lakota women's traditional dance with her niece.

Stella Pretty Sounding Flute and Cecilia Montgomery are frailer now but their spirits remain strong. They are community organizers and activists; they share their knowledge in schools, teach traditional arts, help raise grandchildren, and take pride in their spiritual and cultural traditions. From the grandmothers I have learned more about Lakota and Dakota culture, and myself, than I ever thought possible. This book is just one way of thanking them for all that they have given me.

Celane Not Help Him

CELANE NOT HELP HIM, *a Lakota, was the granddaughter of Iron Hail, who survived the Battle of Little Big Horn and the Wounded Knee Massacre of 1890. From 1985 to 1990 she helped organize the Chief Big Foot Memorial Ride commemorating the one hundred-year anniversary of the massacre. For seven years she volunteered as a disc jockey at community-based radio station KILI in Porcupine, South Dakota. Born on December 25, 1928, she passed away in December 1998 at the age of sixty-nine.*

Every time I come to this place [Wounded Knee Cemetery] it brings back lots of sad memories. Before the Sitanka Wokiksuye Ride [Chief Big Foot Memorial Ride] I can't even think about what happened here; I can't even talk about it. After the Wiping of Tears [Ceremony], I'm brave enough to talk because looks like I could take a deep breath and start thinking ahead. I can look forward; looks like the door's open, encourage me to go on.

Before, when I pass by Wounded Knee, I always go by crying, and then leave crying because what happened here's not easy. It's over a hundred years ago but still it look like it happened yesterday. Lot of people say it's the Battle of Wounded Knee. It's not a battle, it's a massacre. That's what Grandpa told us. I heard it, I grow up with it and it's not easy.

The Seventh Cavalry, they were looking for Sitting Bull. It's not white people that killed him; he's been killed by Indian police. Then the Sitting Bull Band, part of it went to Big Foot and some went into Canada.

In the meantime, Red Cloud told Big Foot to come to Pine Ridge and they could help them settle down. They started out from the Cheyenne River; right along there is a place called Pedro. Twenty-third [December 1890] is when they start.

On the way coming from Bridger [Pedro] some of them were barefoot; they don't have no shoes, and some carry their blankets in strips and wrap their feet, and put moccasins on. They don't eat hot meal; they eat dry meat and drink water. They don't sleep that much, and they always spread out their tipi and sleep under there with the children. The men sleep under the stars.

Some of those old people are blind, and all those children that were on the Big Foot Band, they're hungry too, and they're tired, and they're cold. Grandpa said when they carry their babies in the back, their babies okay but the mothers, their blankets were covered with ice from breathing. The mothers are weak because they nurse their babies and they don't eat that much. It's just pitiful, just terrible. When I talk about it I cry.

Big Foot was really sick and here they came far as Wounded Knee, between Wounded Knee and Porcupine, and he said, "Be careful, there's some horseback [riders] coming at us. They might be from Red Cloud."

But they came and they was from Seventh Cavalry and he [a soldier] asked Big Foot, "Can you talk? I want to see you."

"Yes," he said, "what do you want to see me about?"

He [the soldier] said they need to camp and then have a meeting. So that's when they went down to Wounded Knee.

When they first captured Big Foot and his Band, he told them not to pick fight. "Wait and be humble," he said, "do what you're told. If I'm not sick like this, we could even escape but the reason why I don't want you to start trouble is there's a lot of old people, there's a lot of children."

After they put up their tipi, they [the soldiers] gave them rations: hard-tack and coffee, and sugar, and meat, and rice. They were happy about it because they're starving, and tired, and cold. So they cook and they eat supper.

Right after supper they call Grandpa to go to the Big Foot tent. Grandpa said, "You put on pajamas and comfortable dresses and go to bed. But in those days we have to fix our moccasins too. We have long-legged moccasins, insulation is red grass; we fix those up and then we go to bed and anything happens, we just get up and go. Back in those days it's wild days."

So he was fixing his moccasins and somebody knock on the tipi. He said, "Come in," and here it's an Indian soldier. "We want you to go and sit with Big Foot, keep him company. We're going to take you over there."

He put his coat on and he came out. They go so far and that's when that white soldier shove him and jerk him, but he remember what Big Foot say, "Don't get mad right away and don't pick fight." So he go along with that Indian soldier and white soldier. He went into the tent where Big Foot is; he was laying there. His wife was in there. They were talking and they bring five more and altogether there were six of them. Right now I only remember three person; my grandfather Dewey Beard, and Iron Eyes, and Spotted Thunder. (I heard this when I was little, about eleven, nine years old.) Grandpa Beard was about eighteen or nineteen, and his father, old man Horn Cloud, was forty-four years old.

They sit there all night with Big Foot and they [the soldiers] don't let them sleep, not even lay down for a while, and when they move, they poke them with a gun and told them to sit still. They were sitting like that till morning, and two soldiers came and told them to go and eat and come back again. So he went back to the tent. His wife already cooked, and he told her, "After this meeting we're going to head out to Pine Ridge. Get ready and get the horses ready."

Night before this massacre, those Seventh Cavalry soldiers were drunk all night, Grandpa said. They even shoot a gun out towards tipi; good thing it didn't hit anyone! My [great] grandfather Joe Horn Cloud could understand English, so they ask him to go over there and find out; he went back to the Big Foot tent and he said, "One of the soldiers discharged the gun by itself but nothing happened, don't worry." And that next morning they did that massacre; they kill them all.

He [Dewey Beard] said, "They told us to sit in circle. Before the meeting starts this soldier wants twenty-five guns. We might not even have that much gun; only bow and arrow, that's all we have. This Black Coyote, he can't hear very good but he could talk; he come from the east part of the circle and he said, 'I want everyone to see this. I thought they told us to put our weapons down when we get to Pine Ridge. This might be a trick. Something wrong could happen. I want you to see this. I use this to kill four-legged, feed my family; I don't shoot two-legged with this gun.' And he was going out in the center. Just then a soldier came from the south and one came from the north, and they grabbed the gun but this man was strong so he kind of took it away. So they're all bent down and straighten up towards the south and that gun discharged by itself. He didn't kill nobody. That's when that shooting start and you can't hardly see nothing because of the smoke. When I looked towards my father [Horn Cloud], I was running that way and here I got shot in the leg and in the meantime they're all laying down. They were the first ones to go. They kill them all."

So he [Dewey Beard] have to stay down in the draw cause they're still shooting. One old lady said, "Grandson, don't go out there; whoever moves around they shot them, so hide and don't move." So he was running and all of a sudden he saw his wife. Grandpa Beard's wife has a blanket and has little bit of red in it. He recognize that blanket, and looks like there's a black piece of cloth swinging in front of the face. A woman came and got the baby. His wife shot two places.

He got shot four times; on his back left side on the shoulder blade into his lung, and right below kidney, and on his leg, and on his lap. He look and there's blood all over. He can't even walk normally; he had to drag his feet. Looks like he's going to die, and he doesn't want to stand up but it's getting dark and really cold. He thought, "Maybe I'll just go up and die over there." And he was going up that hill out towards Pine Ridge and he was singing. "I'll sing this death song, and I don't care if they come and kill me." He was walking up and he met three horse-backs and he said, "Now, I'm gone." And here all the time they're Indi-ans, Sioux from Pine Ridge.

So they said, "Are you Lakota?" and he said, "Yes, I'm from that mas-sacre. I'm going up that hill." And one guy said, "Get in the front, in the saddle." Grandpa said, "No I'll sit in the back." They took him so far and there's a cabin. It has a stove in it and a lamp, and no one's there. So they went in and start the fire and make some hot water and take his clothes off; his clothes were stiff with blood. [One of them] got extra clothes on so he put it on him, take him back to Pine Ridge, and already there's about fifteen of them there. Then each morning, he said, every morning, one of them died.

My grandfather and grandma and great-great grandfather were all killed at Wounded Knee. After the massacre, Grandmother Earth covered them with a white blanket; everything was covered with snow. Those frozen bodies lay there three days and they [the soldiers] just pick them up and throw them in that trench over there, and no-body didn't even pray or anything; not even a pipe carrier come around.

It's all right if they wrapped them up at least with a blanket, or sheet and buried them like a human being but Grandpa said they just throw them in there. Some of them were froze, so some of the soldiers step in there and tramp them down to put some more in. They bury all of them in that one place.

He said there's about a fifteen or seventeen-year-old boy—I think he got wounded—and he could live if they only help him but they didn't help him. He opened his eyes but when you're half froze, well, there's nothing you can do. He can't scream or anything, he just open his eyes, look at them but they throw him in there and they bury him alive. When he [Dewey Beard] tell us that he really feel bad; he always have tears in his eyes.

Ever since they killed Sitting Bull, that's where that broken Sacred Hoop starts. Indians used to be in a circle; Sitting Bull, Big Foot and there's another one, and another one [gesturing to points in a circle]. Since they killed Sitting Bull, and then Big Foot, then the sacred hoop was shattered. What can we do to mend this sacred hoop? What I want to do is follow their tracks, follow their ghost trail, road of no return.

I dreamed that I was doing something and Grandpa Beard, and White Lance [his brother] were coming, and I can see there are three more men there but I can't recognize them. Grandpa said, "I want you to just go ahead and do what you planned for December twenty-nine [date of the Wounded Knee Massacre]. You and Birgil [Kills Straight, Celane's cousin] go to Takini [Bridger]. Have a meeting with other survivors over there and bring out your plans and talk to them. They don't need to be scared, we'll watch over. We'll be in the back, and front, and on the sides, and no need to be afraid to get lost because there's animals that will show you the trails."

And I never have a dream that clear. If you dream about something like that you have to remember. And that dream I could remember clear. Next morning I got up and I was thinking, "Maybe for real this is gonna happen; we have to work together and we need help. I wonder who would offer to help?"

I called Birgil but they said he went to Europe. Little by little I saved money and get gas money ready so when he comes back I'm going to ask him to go to Bridger. I think it was Friday morning he called. "I got your message," he said. "I was getting ready to go out in the country and check on my horses. What is it?"

"It's about a dream," I said, "I had a dream."

And he says, "You know, that's what Martin Luther King said." And he said, "It's something big, really important."

"Yes," I said, "this is really important!"

Birgil and me are really close. So I told him that I have that dream and he said, "I had the same dream. You and I will go Bridger and visit the Big Foot camp."

We went over there; he took his tobacco and I took some spirit food. Then we went back to Bridger, and we visit several people and they said he's gonna get help. Here they get together, talk about it and they put on this Memorial Ride of Big Foot Band when they go to Pine Ridge and got killed at Wounded Knee.

Some white people stingy with their land—no trespassing, they got big signs on it. We had a meeting in Phillip [with] the owner of that little store. He said, "I won't be stingy with my land because it's just a pass-through. That history is all over the world and the people will come and see. I'll be proud if I were you." But the people that live on top of the hill, that guy is something else; no mercy.

He said, "Get the hell out of my land! I don't want no damn Indians cross my land. There's a road," he said, "Why do you want to cross my land?"

They told us not to say nothing but I pray. I drop some tobacco ties there and asked the spirits to make him understand what we're trying to do. We didn't say nothing, we just go on the road.

At first there were only nineteen of them, one woman. First night they had ceremony, and they pray for guidance and protection. Right by that Big Foot School, that's where they stay; not any kind of shelter, just make a fire and some put their bedding there and keep their horses there. But with prayers you feel that you're okay, looks like spirits keep you warm or encourage you. They fast four days and four nights. Second year, same thing. That time there are more riders. Third year was more riders. Fourth year was more. Fifth year, oh, there's whole bunch of them! Reason why they were on the ride till 1990, cause they're still in sorrow, mourning; they still remember the person that died. They pray for them, so maybe after this hundred years, they might rest. They are mending the circle, the sacred hoop.

So every time I come here it's a sad memory and it's not easy; and in that mass grave, Grandpa said over four hundred people are buried here; babies and elderly, everybody. When you see those soldiers, it looks like they're really proud. Army got Medal of Honor. They kill old people, and sick men, and babies, and they're really proud. When I think about this I don't care if I get killed by a gun; my father died of heart attack, my grandparents, great-great-grandfather got killed by a bullet. That's how I want to go; I don't want to get sick and taken to the hospital and given IV's and everything.

The soldiers had black souls and black hearts. If I live to be a thousand I won't forget, and when I'm gone my children and then my grandchildren will remember.

That tombstone, memorial monument, it's got the names on; my grandfather's, Chief Big Foot and his wife, Horn Cloud; all four sides it has names on it. Even if I'm homeless, even if I have nothing, I'm going to live around here. I'm not going to leave because my grandfather, grandmother, all buried here.

That's all I can tell you.

I was born December 25, 1928, out in Grass Creek between Manderson and Oglala. My grandfather Dewey Beard—his Indian name in English, Iron Hail, and in Indian, Wasu Maza. My grandmother name is Alice Tasunka Opi Win, or Wounded Horse. One Bear, that's her maiden name, and my father name is Webster Sherman Beard. On my mother's side my grandfather's name is Charlie Kills Enemy, and his wife maiden name is Rose Half Rope. My mother name is Agnes Martha Kills Enemy.

My father died when I was fourteen months old and I was raised by my grandparents in Red Water Creek. When we lived there we got a big horse ranch. We have a little over a thousand head of horses, and a few cattles and chickens. We have a big garden, our own corn field and al-falfa field, and hay fields. Then we got two log house and one frame house; the frame house is still there, the barn and the corral.

[During] World War II, the aerial ground gunnery range, the Air Force, took over that whole strip where we live. We have to move out of there within thirty days. At first they say forty-five days; later on we got a letter from the War Department, only thirty days because the war's getting worse. We had only four head of horses out of that thousand head; we lost everything. So that's why I say Grandpa got massacred two times by army; first, at that Wounded Knee, and second time [when] we have to move out of that place for the Air Force.

Then later they said you'll get your land back, and I thought they going to return it to the individual owners but instead they turn it over to the tribe. I check over there and they want more than $400; we have to have that much to deposit but I haven't got that kind of money. So it belongs to the tribe now and I don't have a home.

For thirty-nine years I've been waiting for a house but every time I go to the Tribal Housing Authority they say, "There's more than 100 people waiting before you." So that's tough. They always tell me I'm as poor as snake, but at least snake has a hole to live in. I don't have that. We plant some cedars and pines up on the hill and they're still there. The family will be buried up there. When I go there it brings back a lot of memories.

It's good to have been raised by grandparents. Grandpa Beard never go to school but he's a smart man; he had a lot of patience with us, and Grandma's like that too. They know what's right and what's wrong; they got values and they set you straight.

Grandpa and Grandma don't believe in punish the little ones. Grandma said, "Looks like it's going to be a snow storm. When that snow cover all those chips it won't have any kindling." She told me to rake some of those chips, and pile them up and cover them, and fill up all the water containers. But we got some new puppies. I liked them and so I feed them and I really have fun. I pet them; they're cute.

"Hey," she called me, "Celane, did you finish rake?"

"Oh gee, Grandma, I forgot. I'll do it right now." Got my mittens on and I rake up the leaves. Then I got the buckets to go after some water and she said, "I want to tell you something. Stop for a minute. You know what?" she said. "You can turn into snake by not listening to grandparents. There's a story to that one."

"Grandma, I want to hear that." She said, "Get done with all your chores, I'll tell you."

So I got the water and I fill up all the containers and pile them up and cover them with chips and I came back inside. "Okay, Grandma, can you tell me now?" and she said, "Wait, I'm cooking supper." So I'm really anxious to hear. I want her to tell me now but she said, "If I tell you now you won't remember part of it so after supper, after we eat."

"Alright." I set the table and I'm really good, I'm really nice. I want to hear that story. After we eat, Grandpa said, "I want to go out and check around, make a fence ride."

So after supper I really want to hear. She said, "Wait till you wash dishes." I wash dishes and then Grandpa came back and she told him that she's going to tell me a story about three boys turning to snake by not listen to what they've been told. So Grandpa said, "That's a good idea. That's one of the good stories. Listen close and try and remember everything because one week later, I'm going to ask you and see if you can remember everything."

She said, "Back in those days when the boys had a strong grip so they could shoot with the bow and arrow, they were going on a training. There's seven big boys, and eleven-year-old on down; altogether there's eleven of them. They stay three nights. First night, they all work real good. They all help each other making three grass huts; two big ones and a small one. This chief, this grandpa that goes with them, instruct them what to do. When it's daybreak they start going.

"All day they were walking and that evening, again, they work real good. They make grass hut and some went down to creek to get water, and make fire. Now the third day, he told them to build a grass hut kind of fast [because] it's getting dark and three boys don't want to do it.

"'We've been working hard all this time, so we're going to rest,' and they were laying around. He begged them to help but they don't do it. One of them came and he ask this chief, 'Grandpa, can we go and check around that lake over there?'

"He [the grandpa] said, 'That lake, before you get to half-ways, it's going to be dark because that lake is pretty big.'

"But they said, 'We're just going to go anyway. Why do we listen to him? Come one, let's go!' So they went to check around there.

"I bet they didn't even go around that lake; they came back with nice piece of meat and they show it to the man. They said, 'We don't have to go down and hunt for rabbits or prairie chickens or anything for supper, we've got piece of meat.'

"He said, 'Where did you get that?' and they said, 'We found it over there.'

"'Maybe it's not good, just leave it over there,' he said.

"'No, it's good meat. Well, since you don't want it, we'll eat it.' They slice it, and on open fire they fry the meat, and they eat it. They were laying around and they didn't even do anything.

"That evening, he sent some boys down to the river to get some rabbits and game. They brought some up and they fried them. 'While we fry our meat,' he said, 'we're going to talk, have a council.' They ask those boys to come around and listen. And he said, 'I have to count on you four boys to be security till midnight, and then after midnight, there'll be four more,' and he told them which direction to go.

"When they got done eating the securities went out. That boy up north, he's supposed to whistle to these boys but he forgot. He look up and here that star went by way over. It's after twelve. 'Hey, I'd better whistle.' He whistled to this one, he whistled to that one, so they all going back to that grass hut. They go so far and someone's crying and here, it's in one of those big boys' grass hut. He opened the grass hut and he jumped back; he's scared of something. 'Hey come here! Come and see this!'

"So they all came out, and already two of those boys turn into big snakes. And this one right beside the door, half of his body turning to snake but he could cry and he could talk. So he said, 'I won't turn into snake right away but I'm going to be like this for a while so I'm going to tell you something. When they told you something, do it. By not listening, this is what happened to us. You see, they're already turn into snake and they can't make sound. When you go back to our relatives, tell them exactly what happened. In a little while, I'm going to turn into a snake but we're going to live in that lake till the end of the world. Tell mother, ina, to bring me wasna [pemmican] if she's going to come see me. Tell everyone what happened to us.' He was crying, he wish he listened to what the chief told him. Then he turn into snake; he got tears in his eyes. So they follow each other into that water, Devil's Lake.

"So they went back, and they told the parents, and everyone's crying. So later on, grandmas, and aunts, and moms, they make wasna and take it to the Devil's Lake. This boy's mother went to the bank and she called her son. She said, 'Cinks, son, I got the message so I bring you the wasna. Come close if you can hear me.'

"And here, in a little while, looks like there's a stump came out of the water, and here it's that big snake. So she throw wasna at him and he got it and went back in the water. After that you can see a bunch of stumps all over. They came. She threw wasna at them and they took off."

Grandma said, "That Devil's Lake is there long time and it's going to be there until the end of the world. Now you don't listen, you're going to turn into snake." Two weeks later, Saturday evening at the supper table, Grandpa said, "Did you remember what Grandma told you about that story? I want you to tell me." So I told him and he said, "You got good brain, you listen and I'm glad. Remember that. Don't let it slip away from you. One of these days we're going to be gone, and if you forget about this story," he said, "you're lost." So ever since then, when they told me something, I try to remember, and I don't want to turn into snake, so when they told me to do something, I do it right away, and do it real good.

In our lives, traditional ways is another thing you have to learn and you have to understand; respect the elderly, and parents, and the sacred pipe. White Buffalo Woman was the one that brought our sacred pipe, Ptehincala Cannunpa, the Calf Pipe. There's a story to it but since I'm a sundancer, and I fast, and I pierce, I have to be careful what I tell.

The white people's side they have a Bible and a cross, and Ten Commandments. On the traditional side they have rules. The sweat lodge is always the first one to do, purify yourself. Grandpa said they told them to unwrap that sacred pipe in the mid part of summer. All the people could go over there and pray, and maybe sundance or fast. Like nowadays, right after sundance they drink beer and stuff but back in those days you have be real careful, purify yourself all through the year and then visit the sacred pipe.

Grandpa always told me that when I was young. He said, "We never get paid for doing things. We help each other, we cooperate and that's how we get things going easier. Nowadays, you have to put in time and they'll pay you whatever. Back in those days it's fun. Like if it's time to build a shade for the sundance, we all get together and build a shade. Or if there's a sweat, we'll all get together and get wood and have sweat. There's a fast, we all help this person that's going to go out in the hills, cut the cherry trees for the flags. Something happen, death in the family, we all take food over there and stay with them, take what good things we have." He said, "Sharing is our business. We let each other know that we care for each other. It's not the same person that's going to pay you but the Great Spirit will choose somebody to give you help."

Looks like [I] think I'm a queen. This car came by. "Oh, where are you going?"

"I'm going to Rushville."

"Get in! You going to walk all this way?"

I get in. I always think there's good people around. I went to Rushville. Then I got my business done and I was heading out this way and the same pickup stop by. "Are you going back?" and I said, "Yes, I have to get home," and I got a ride. I was going to the telephone office and then Pat pulled in. "What are you doing over here?"

"I'm going to the telephone office, I want to have my phone turned on."

"Get in, I'll take you." So it's fast, I didn't thumb. I'm happy as a clown, phone ringing for first time in so many days.

KILI [community radio station] was looking for volunteers. I talked to Dorothy [a friend] and she said, "Let's do it. It's not going to hurt us."

We've been through four trainings. First three years we go in at six o'clock in the morning, so from here we start out at four o'clock. We got there about five and we turn on the power. If it's wintertime we have to turn on the de-icer one hour before and warm everything up. Then try out the meters and when the register's good you play the grand entry song, the Indian national anthem, and then prayer. Then play Lakota music, tell the time, and every hour, station ID. Then PSA's and swap shop, birthday request, memorial request. Lakota music has a honoring song; there's soldier's honoring song, deceased [honoring song] and all that. You have to be careful with that, you have to play the right kind! [laughs] There's woman's honoring song, and woman's traditional song, and jingle dress songs.

I told my daughter Marie, "Get into that training and be one of those volunteer DJ's, micunksi [my daughter], because it's good." She's a DJ and play oldie goldies, and my granddaughter, Summer, she play rap music, and then we play Indian powwows.

We're volunteer DJ's for eight years. They call us "golden girls." Dorothy got a car. We use that car until it give out. That was in April so we start hitchhiking. Ever since then we go every Sunday afternoon. We always catch a ride. Sometimes it's hard because during the wintertime the days are short and by the time we get to Wounded Knee it's dark.

Then sometimes we thumb. A lot of people recognize us. They give us a ride but sometimes [it's a] rough ride with the drunkards. [laughs] Sometimes we ride in the back of the pickup and when it's getting cold we have to put more clothes on. It's fun and it's funny! While I'm able to do things I will do it, and then when I'm disabled and everything, I'll remember those.

I remember a lot of things I heard. Grandpa Big Foot, and Sitting Bull, and Crazy Horse, they're close relatives. My grandfather Horn Cloud and Big Foot are first cousins, and so is Sitting Bull.

Grandpa said when Crazy Horse was a young boy, they like to go out riding. Maybe three go out, and during summer they stay someplace, or during the winter when it's cold they learn to survive. During March they went out riding. They told them not to go too far because early spring, horses tire out real easy. Crazy Horse rode a buckskin color horse and he got tired; pretty soon he wouldn't even go any more. So Crazy Horse told those two others to go back and he said he could have his horse graze a little bit and rest.

At first he went into the pines and canyon right there. He put his horse to graze and he tried to go to sleep but he said, "What if somebody got on the horse?" So he went up, and he was sitting by a big pine tree and pretty soon he went to sleep. He really sleep and I guess he hears a noise. He opens his eyes and was laying there. "Where am I? Oh, I remember I was out here." He went back to sleep again, and he dreamed that a man was singing over the hill somewheres and he was coming. He was dressed in buckskin and he had two feathers back there [in his hair], and he was looking at him for a long time and was singing. He didn't come to him right away. He was looking around, back and forth, and he came over. "Hoksila," he said, "Boy, what are you doing here? What happened?"

Crazy Horse said, "My horse is tired so I have to stay here. He's over there." He turned around and he looked at the horse but the horse still eating. He talked to him about a lot of things but I can't tell what that man said to this boy; it's a secret, not supposed to tell. He talked to him and he said, "I'm going to tell you this. Your horse is okay. When you get up, ride him and go home but remember what I told you. When you get home your father can help you.

"Your horse is giving you a hard time. If it was someone else, he could leave that horse and go home, but I know you like your horse. You don't want to lose it so that's why you're staying here; sleep out under the stars, no blankets or nothing." From that he gave him a name; he said since he's got a crazy horse that his name's going to be "Crazy Horse." That name's going to be big wherever he goes. He said, "If you carry that thing I told you to carry, no bullet can hurt you but always remember to do what I told you to do. Now I'm going."

He turn around and go back so far, and all of a sudden this man jumped and sat down, and he turned himself into a jack rabbit. (I don't know what they call those jack rabbits, their ear points are black.) He jumped around and was running and go back over the hill. There's a song to it but I can't sing, I'm not supposed to.

So Crazy Horse got up and was standing around and look at his horse but he was still grazing. "Maybe he's thirsty, I should go home." He got on, and oh, that horse was just brand new. He went home, and on the way going back there's three horseback [riders] coming. He went down the draw and he went back up and they just came over real fast and they said, "Where have you been? We're looking for you. Your mom's worry about you." They hug him. "We're glad you're okay."

Crazy Horse father had [had] a ceremony and he wants the spirits to watch over him wherever he is. They told him Crazy Horse was over seven hills right by a canyon but they didn't tell him a man came to him. So that's where he got his name. It's a simple name but then it's a brave man. And that's all I can tell you.

Grandpa and Grandma always tell me, "Wherever you live, and whatever you live in, even if it one-room shack, or tent, or tipi, take care of it and try to make it look pretty and nice. Reason why is because you live there and you can do anything you want; sleep long time, or sew, or raise your kids in there, and it represents your mother."

There's about three stories about the tipi. I'll tell you a little bit about what happened. They said we used to live in a cave; I can just see myself live in a cave! They used to come out, and the men used to hunt deer and buffalo, and then they go back in the cave. One time they came out and here it was green grass and really pretty. They want to stay out over night. They did, and when they try to go back to find that cave, they can't find it, they're lost. So they were out a long time.

Back in those days, they said, we don't have very many clothes on. Some man said he had a dream and he told his people to get all the hides they can and dry them. He told them to divide them up and the men will take some on one side of the hill, and the women take some on the other side. "One month you come back over here, we'll meet."

I guess this woman had a dream that she fixed dresses somehow, and so they make themselves buckskin dresses. And that man had a dream; knows how to make those leggings and breechcloth. One month [later] they came back and they were all dressed.

This woman dreamed; maybe Grandmother Earth, she's the one that come to this woman and told her, "You're not going to go back to the cave but you're going to live in a tipi"— she didn't say "tipi" then, "something you're going to live in," she said.

"That little tipi," she said, "it's just like a mother sitting on the ground. See her dress; the hem is where you stake it down. The tipi has fourteen poles; each one represents something, and what it's made out of is from sacred animal, and the pole come from the Mother Earth.

And then when you go in, it's just like your mother." She [the woman] told the people and that's when they make those buffalo-hide tipi.

"We live in a tipi when I was a little girl." Grandma told us that. And she said, "Back in those days, grandmas sleep by the door and if there's a grandma lost her husband, they both sleep by the door. When someone goes out she knows, and when someone comes in she knows that someone's coming in, and when they all sleep she close the door and go to sleep.

"Early in the morning Grandma gets up and she make pot of soup, pot of food. When we get up, we all get up in a circle. We see each other, we know each other; we know when someone's sick. We're very close, the families. Back in those days nobody eat fancy or nobody go hungry because we eat from the same pot, everyone, every family; and if ones don't have that much food then we share. So living in a circle is a good life."

They always camp in a circle. When all the different nations get together in summertime, they have certain directions; like Hunkpapa they live west side of the circle and there's Minneconju and all those. They get together during the summer and first thing they do is they sundance and fast. After that they have naming ceremony, adoption ceremonies, or things like that. Then they have that kind of fair, like horse races and foot races; and in evenings they have social dances and give-aways. Then during fall, when the leaves turn brown, they scatter all directions until next spring again.

I rode in horse race; I didn't win anything. When we live in Red Water I rode horses a lot, even if it's a wild horse. They're all the same, tame and wild, pretty soon I'm not scared. If a horse is going to buck, or what a horse has in his or her mind, looks like I know.

Grandpa told me to get the team across the creek. I was walking towards the corral and there's a horse there right in the middle tied up. I opened the corral gate and went towards that horse; the horse was kind of nervous. I said, "Hey, what are you doing here? Let's go get the horses," and I got on. Here it looks like he kind of bunched up and was barely walking.

"What's wrong with you?" I said. I go out there to get the team and I chased them into the creek and let them drink water. Grandpa was standing out there with oats and he rattled that thing so they ran over there.

I tied the horse up and I was coming back and Grandpa said, "What are you doing over there?"

"Well, you told me to get the team so there they are."

"And you ride that horse?" he said.

I said, "Yeah, that's the only one that's out there.

Grandpa said, "I mean that one in the barn!"

So my uncle, Ben Morrison—his name is Conquering Bear, and he can't talk but he sign language—point at me and he said, "You're brave." I didn't know what to say. I just hold my head down and went back in the house.

"Oh jeez, I done something wrong," and Grandma said, "What is it?" I said, "I rode a horse, and Grandpa said that that horse never been rode before."

So that's why I said, wild horse and tame one, they're all the same.

Back when Grandpa was a little boy, he always told us that they eat meat boiled, you know; no bread, no salt, no sugar, no coffee, just meat and soup. Sometimes they dry meat and then pound on it and make wasna. Papa is this dry meat; you put it in a big pan of water and let it soak for a while. Then you pound on it till it's nice and fluffy. You have to have kidney fat; fry it and get the grease and put sugar in, or chokecherry to sweeten the wasna. You have to pound on it real fine and mix it and make it into balls. That's travelling food they always say. When they go on the warpath, long trip or something, they carry those.

Grandpa always say, "Which food is good for your body?" [laughs] I'm anxious to answer but my cousin answer, "Vegetable and milk. The teacher told us that; told us to drink a lot of milk and eat a lot of vegetable." He look at us and he said, "Let me tell you something; we're going to try this tonight. Let's put out a vegetable and a piece of meat outside"—it was in winter—"and we'll see which one we could use again."

So he put out the meat and the vegetable. Next morning, I'm anxious to see which one we could use again. So I was thinking, "Oh-oh, the vegetables are all frozen." I said, "I think the meat."

"You're right," he said, "you freeze the meat you can use it again but look [at the] vegetable. That's how your body going to be. You're going to freeze easy. By drinking lot of milk you get lazy, and when somebody talk to you, you sit there lowered and look like a cow." Oh God, what shall we tell the teacher when we go back to school? Which food is good for you? [laughs]

Grandma Beard teach me how to bead and do quill work. Quill work is one thing that if I have to do it I will but I'm not really interested in it. I don't want to have to chase porcupines. I'm scared of porcupines. [laughs] They lift their tail up and swing it somehow so it shoots out [quills] and when it gets in your skin, it's really hard to get it out and it gives you infection. So what Grandma does is she'd throw a blanket on that porcupine and got the quills out; keep on doing that until the porcupine got tired and she let it go. I can't do that; that's risky. What if some landed on my forehead?

I'm interested in make quilts. That person who showed me and teach me how to make star quilts is long gone; Lucy Kills Straight, that's Birgil Kills Straight's mother, my aunt. First we start out with squares, and when we make quilt squares, we sew them together and make it big. I made a mistake. Mine was big one side and smaller this way and I don't want to show it to her. I know what she's going to say; she's going to make me rip it and sew it over again. So I show it to her and she said, "That's the first thing you make and so we'll just keep it like that, we'll put lining on it, and you'll use it but later on you're going to have to make a real good one." Oh, I was so happy when she told me that. "Oh good, auntie." And then later on she showed us how to make designs.

I make my own designs; turtle, and war bonnets, and I'm going to make Chief Sitting Bull; I saw his picture. And then the buffalo skull, and that buffalo design, and eagle, lone star, broken star, and falling star. Sometimes, if you put the right colors together, when you look at it from a distance, looks like it moves. Right now I'm making quilts; lately we have three deaths in the family. We have to stay up all night and quilt. They have to have something to cover the coffin, so I volunteer my fingertips for a while.

I learned how to tan hides from my grandma Alice Beard and her older sister Sally Staber. Grandma Beard showed me how to tan deer hide, and antelope, and Grandma Staber show me how to make smoked hide; she use a corn cob and cotton tree leaves. Grandma Staber is the one that teach me how to tan cow hide; you have to scrape it first. "Do it in old ways," she always said, "not in new ways." That's what Grandma said too. "Put too much salt in it, it stains and it dries out, and when it dries up it's no good anymore." So that's what I'm going to do to that cow-hide over there, do it the old way.

Deer hide, you soak it and then pull out the hair as much as you could and then scrape the rest. Then stake it a little bit and when it dries up, you put oil on it, or grease. We always use bacon grease or that kidney fat, and you tend it. I got those side blades that you work it with, back and forth. Then you turn it over, all directions, and it spreads out but you have to work it before it gets too dry. When you put it away you wet double layer of towel and wrap it around so it won't get dry, and then you work it again. So you learn things like that and always remember how to do it. What you learn, nobody can take away from you.

My grandmother said her aunt, she's a medicine woman. Late at night when there's a medicine she has to dig, she go way out where nobody is. Grandma says she sings and she prays, and she called this medicine's name. She could see it just like a glow in the dark. She took it and bring it back and leave it hang outside. She's [the] only one who could do that but she died. Grandma don't want to do it. I ask her, tried to make her show me and she said, "No, that's her power, that's hers. She's gone, she took it with her."

I went to school at Holy Rosary Mission for three years. Holy Rosary is just like a army camp; you have to do this right on time and on the double, and you're not supposed to talk Indian, which is hard. I want to talk Indian sometimes. If we talk Indian they punish us. They slap us in the mouth, or hit us in the mouth with a ruler! I told Grandpa Beard and he says, "I think the priest or sisters might think you're saying something bad, or you plan to do something bad. That's why they don't want you to talk Indian and so do what you're told."

But sometimes when the old lady come and wants us to interpret for her, it's really good to interpret for her; big fat chance to talk Indian, your own language. I was so happy to see her. [laughs] Sometimes they [the elderlies] came there to buy roast beef, and that old lady she don't know how to say that in English. I always run over there to her.

"Grandma, what do you want? Do you want me to interpret for you?" I wanted to, and in Indian I said, "Unci, taku yacin he? Iyeciciska kte?" She said, "Han, yes. I came to buy bread and a piece of roast. " So looks like I'm tricky. Grandpa told me not to talk Indian but I'm going to talk Indian. [laughs] Up to this day when Grandpa died, [I think] "I shouldn't do that." I really feel bad but I guess helping another person that don't know how to talk English, I shouldn't get punished for that.

I think it's better if you talk your own language. I can't talk perfect English but I can make the white people understand me. It's hard.

There's a lot of change between when your grandparents talk Indian to you all the time and in the Indian ways; it's more comfortable to me but when I go to the white man's world [laughs] I have to be careful with a lot of things.

The teachers, and brothers, and sisters, are pretty strict. Sometimes they punish us; they make us go to bed without supper. That's one thing, they'll starve you. Just like the government said, "You sign the treaty or starve." That's how it is; you don't do it, you'll starve. They think that food could lead us around but after a while I'm used to it. During that time it's WW II and so if we leave some leftovers on the table, that next meal we don't eat. So that's where I learned to get a piece of bread and clean my plate. My plate is shiny; it looks like it's never been used. It's unbelievable when I think about it now.

We went to church but I don't know how to pray. "I believe in God, Hail Mary, Holy Mary," we have to say those, and we tell our sins. If we're really good, they give us five Hail Mary's to say. If we're bad they give us fifty Hail Mary's but for long time I can't understand. Grandpa pray with the sacred pipe, or go to sweat lodge. Grandpa always say, "Great Spirit make everyone; Lakota people come from the Great Spirit and he loves all of them." So that's what I believe but when I go to Catholic school I have to keep praying and don't sin. "If you sin, your heart's going to be this color," and she call it a "'black heart' and that leads you like a fire down to hell; you live with the devil. You're not going to see God, you're not going to see Jesus either."

At first I don't know who Jesus is and I ask a girl. "I don't know either but you know that's Papa Jesus," she said. One of them told me,

"That's your big brother and God is your father. He made you." One time I got confused because one sister call my name and asked, "Who made you?"

I really don't know what I'm going to say. "My father."

"Who is your father?"

"Webster Beard but he died, I guess him," I said. I got punished for saying that. Kids don't understand too good but when you're treated like that, it makes it worse; you're afraid to answer.

I always seen Grandpa pray with the pipe; then I go to Holy Rosary and looks like I lost everything but one day I pick up somewheres, get back. I believe in the traditional way, the sacred pipe. That's why I say you can't be a white woman if you're born Lakota and you can't be an Indian when you're wasicun win, [a white woman]. Nowadays it went back the other way. Priests pray with the sacred pipe too, and they want to learn the Lakota language. That makes me sick, just like my stomach growl. I don't think the government know what he wants; he changed a lot.

I stay there till I was in fifth grade. After that I went to Little Wound School [for] three years. From Red Water to Kyle Little Wound School it's seven miles. I have a little saddle horse and early in the morning I just start out. I always carry extra clothes in case there'll be a thunderstorm or something like that. So I rode back and forth, and then when winter comes, I stay at my aunt's house. Three years I've been doing that, and then I have to go to boarding school. I like Pierre Indian School but it's too far; I miss Grandma and Grandpa, miss seeing them.

By then my aunt really got sick and Grandma needs my help because they [her grandparents] work at Cedar Pass. I have to stay and watch auntie. After she pass away, I work several places; Grand Island in defense work and after I got transferred to Igloo Ordnance Depot making ammunition.

Grandma said, "In future you'll find a man but having boyfriend too soon, then you like that boy and all you're waiting for is him. Try to learn all you can, go to school, and work, and do things, and then think about getting married or boyfriend. If your husband is not educated, and he's a lazy guy, and he don't have horses or anything, you're going to have to feed and clothe your children. And some of those boys are like that," she said, "nobody ever tell them anything."

I met Jonas when I was seventeen but still I'm scared what Grandma told me. He always come talk to me but I have other things to do. I avoid it and three years [later] is when we think about getting married but I don't feel good about it. I feel sick. I'll never be free.

We got married in a [meat] locker. [laughs] The justice of the peace that married us owned that locker. We went over there and he was sweeping the floor. He piled up the dirt right there on one side, and on the other side pigs dangling, and some turkeys and chickens. Real good, a sharp one, unique! [laughs]

We live in Rapid City and I live in the air base. When they fixed that fence I was cement finisher, and when they finish those hangers we wash the windows, hanging way out there like a little spider. I work in the cafes, dishwasher, and wait tables. I work at the Sioux San[itarium] Hospital one time. I work eleven years at Cedar Pass Lodge; they used to have a souvenir shop. It's good to earn your own money; you either save it or buy clothes for the little ones, dress them good.

I got five boys and three girls. I know it's really hard to raise that many children but again, it's a lot of experience and being poor is good experience. I'm not ashamed to tell that I'm always poor. [Now] I get $28.50 every two weeks but I don't think it's enough. Sometimes I have to save or go without it. Lately, I apply for ssi, that's $407 a month. But that first check I have to share where I'm staying. I have to help pay gas or electricity, or phone, or food and sometimes I got $3 left. I have to stretch that.

Sometimes, I think back in those days, Grandma and Grandpa never have money in their lives but they're still alive and there's something there that takes care of them. So that comes to my mind and that helps; looks like it encourage me that I really shouldn't be thinking about money.

Grandpa told us, "Being a parent, you have to be strong, wacin nitanka kte. You have to have patience and knowledge. And you have to be brave, cante nit'inzin kte, nahan fortitude. Wa'unsiyala kte [you must have mercy], wacante yagnakin kte [you must have compassion]. You have to have all these."

My first child was born at home; all were born at home except three. Being Indian is hard because when I think about it, the reason I don't want to go to the hospital is I don't want no strange people to see me. My husband's mother helped me several times and Wayne, the fourth of the boys, I delivered myself and it's sacred; with this blizzard you can hardly go no place, you can't get no help.

I told my kids, "Turn off the lights and [leave] just that lamp, and if anyone knock on the door tell them, 'We're not supposed to let any one in,' and close it." So they did; Marie, and Claire, and Dewey. Then my baby comes and I just sat up and cut the cord, and cleaned him up, and wrapped him up. So I deliver one of my son, and he had a lot of patience, he don't get mad, he's special, different from others.

Before the babies come, you make some sage tea and right after the baby's born you wash them with that sage. Grandpa said, "That baby is from a different world. That baby never been in this world before, and when they slip into the world you wash them with the sage because the sage come from the Grandmother Earth. She wants to be the first one to take care of the baby. If you do that, this Grandmother Earth is watching him; make sure that he has a good, clean, quiet life and knowledge. You take him into Lakota family and he's going to be Lakota. There's no way he can change his life to be a wasicun. Wasicun has different ways of life; they don't believe in our traditions.

"After you wash the baby with the sage there's a lotion made out of kidney fat and there's some kind of herb and water. You boil them together and let it settle; you empty the water but have that salve and you put it all over them, and you talk to them.

"'Now you came into this world, and the family will love you and keep you. The Great Spirit send you to us.' You talk to them like that; even if they're just a newborn baby, still it goes in their brains," he said. Some, they don't do that to the babies, so those babies cry a lot, especially when it's getting dark; in the middle of the night the baby's crying.

He said that we're not supposed to hang out children clothes [at night] cause there's a spirit from the east that comes with the darkness and it touch the clothes, and you don't take little ones outside when it's dark because that darkness will change their mind into doing bad things. You have to keep them inside and teach them to come back before dark and stay inside.

So when we were little ones, Grandma always told us to go inside. My grandmother, Alice Beard's aunt, always tell us stories and she told us to say "Han [yes]," and if we don't say that she quit 'cause she knows we go to sleep. She said one time one of us went to sleep but we keep on saying "han" and here she check up on us and she said, "They're all sleeping but in their sleep they're saying 'Han.'"

Grandpa always say, "Teach your kids and talk to them, even if they're babies; that's the time to put a lot of good things in their mind and make sure their heart is developed in a good way. They remember as they grow and go down the Red Road."

When Grandma cook our favorite meal, that's when Grandpa always told us those. I always try to remember what they told me because they're gone, and they'll never tell me again.

That's all I'm going to say.

Stella Pretty Sounding Flute

STELLA PRETTY SOUNDING FLUTE, *a Wahpekute-Hunkpati Dakota, is from the Crow Creek Reservation in South Dakota. She was born on July 20, 1924, in a tent on the banks of the Missouri River with her grandmothers as midwives. As a child she helped her mother and grandmothers gather and dry fruits and medicines and tan hides. Her home in Aberdeen, South Dakota, is a cottage industry for making star quilts. A sewing machine sits in a corner of the kitchen covered in neat stacks of multicolored fabric diamonds, and a quilting frame is folded against one wall when not in use.*

Stella Pretty Sounding Flute grew up in an era when traditional spiritual practices were outlawed by the government. Now a pipe carrier, she helped organize the movement to stop the desecration of the Minnesota pipestone quarries and have them returned to native control. In 1999 she traveled to Costa Rica to attend World Peace and Prayer Day, an international indigenous gathering.

My grandmother used to say, "Ho, takoza, un'a ded iyotaka. Takuku oci-ciyakin kte." That means, "My granddaughter, come here, let me talk to you. I'm going to tell you these things so then you can tell your takoza, your grandchildren."

I used to see her go to rummage [sales] and pick up some plain cloth and cut diamonds by hand, so I used to watch her make quilts. I was about eight, nine, in there. They didn't make too much star quilts in those days when I was growing up because material was hard to get and then when they did get—oh that was just precious! Our grand-mothers didn't want us to touch their material or their threads. They'd have frames and they'd stretch them out and quilt. They put it together all by hand.

The star quilt comes from the stars; that's what my grandmother said. Our ancestors used to watch the heavens, the stars, the moon, and the sun. They would observe them and really study them; the stars are so bright that they sparkle so they call it wicanhpi, a diamond. The star quilt was too sacred to even think about making because them diamonds belonged to God! Then all of a sudden it's coming up and everybody's using it.

The first star quilt that our grandmothers made was four points; one color would be a black point and one color would be a white point, one would be a yellow point, and a red point. Our ancestors used to have the four directions of the four winds, so those were the four-directions star quilts that our ancestor grandmothers used to make, but pretty soon somebody come up with the idea where there's eight points.

Red was the favorite color of our ancestors because red represents the human blood and animals have blood that is red. Our grandmothers thought about making star quilts out of flowers so they represented the Mother Earth colors; there's brown and red and orange and yellow. All of these represent the colors that God made; you see them in the rainbow and the setting of the sun, so I try to imitate what my grandmothers had in mind to design.

When I was young I'd stand there at the frame in the kitchen. I'd tell my husband to put up kerosene lamps and he'd put 'em in the four corners, you know. I'd really be hand stitching! I sewed almost half of the night!

In the wintertime, that's when I hand-quilt because it's easier. I can't go no place, I can't go to Bingo. [laughs] I can't go to wacipis [pow-wows], I can't go to no pipe ceremonies. I just stay home and pray and I do whatever I want to do. So whenever some women come, we come in here and I say, "Put your stitches in there."

I made a lot of star quilts, maybe over a thousand. My star quilts are all over South Dakota, and two went to Germany. I make them to give away, I make them to honor somebody, I give them to cover somebody when they die. So whenever I sit and sew these star quilts, I just wonder who's going to get them.

I'm a full-blood Leaf-Shooter [Wahpekute] and Hunkpati Dakota. My ancestors were the Standing Buffalo and they always camped where there was water, plenty of food, medicine, and shelter along the river.

My Indian name was given by my great-grandparents. My great-grandmother's husband got killed at Little Big Horn; her mother and dad were killed. She traveled along the river on foot; it was time for me to have an Indian name before anything else happens.

It's a sacred name and nobody else has this name and nobody could ever take it away from me. My Indian name is Tahinspa Waste Win; that means "Pretty Quill Woman," and my ancestors, before the white man came, they always used tahinspa, porcupine quills, to decorate whatever they were wearing: moccasins or their buffalo robes or deer hides, deer dresses. They would take these porcupine quills and they would dye them out of the fruit that God put on Mother Earth.

I was born and raised on the Crow Creek Indian Reservation, Fort Thompson, South Dakota. I was born July 20, 1924; it was hot and there was a tent there and that's where my mother was in labor and that's where I was born. Then my grandmothers and her sisters, they rushed to the Missouri River and they dunked me in there when I was just a few minutes old and washed me off, and they used sage and rubbed me off. Then they planned this Indian name for me.

They got a whole buffalo; they skinned it, they aged it and then they cooked it. There was about twenty, thirty, women at a time tending to that buffalo skin so by the time I was going to have my Indian name it was all ready.

Before I was a year old they put me in a buffalo robe and they put this eagle plume on my head, and my ancestor grandmothers told me a lot of things but I was just a baby, maybe a month old. So later on, the things that they told me, well it's coming back to me, so before I die, I will fulfill whatever they requested when they prayed to God, when they pinned this eagle plume on my head. So that's the way I got my Indian name.

Our ancestors, they always believed in the animals, those that fly, the eagles, the swans and the ducks and geese; they would ask for a vision or a dream, then they would pray so that name would come to them. My mother, her name is Hupahu Duta Win; it means "Red Wing Woman." She got that from her ancestors. When she was a small child there would be some birds that would come and they would fly over her. They had red tipped wings so she's named after that. My dad, he swim across the river and visit with his relatives over there and then in the evening, he'd come back. His Indian name was Bde Mani Wicasta; that means "He that Walks with the Water."

You have to carry it [the name], you have to earn it but me I didn't earn it. My grandmothers already predicted my life and so they gave me this Indian name. I made arrangements that if anything should happen to me, my niece—she's traditional like me—she would carry my name.

They didn't have no star quilts but they had sinew and they had leather. They had dried meat, dried corn, and dried cherries and those were the give-aways.

The buffalo, the elk, and the deer were really important to our tribe, the Dakota, Lakota, and Nakota. Way before the white man came, our ancestors had council meetings. They would sit in a circle and share this pipe, they would pray to God first. Then they would say, "Tatanka tonaktca uncinpta he?" What that means is, "How many buffalo are we going to need? Ta'hinea tonaktca uncinpta he? How many deer are we going to need? There's winter coming."

They regarded the eagle as a messenger from God. Our grand-fathers had real strong vision, and this eagle had more vision so they would watch him and then they would go and get a buffalo herd.

Everything that God made was round and they were all circle[s]; the fruit was circle, and the stars were circles, and the moon was circle and the sun was circle, and the world was a circle. It was the world that was moving, so that's where that circle of life comes from. So that's the way our ancestors traveled, in that great circle. A certain grandmother carried the medicine, a certain grandma carried the different kind of teas, and the men carried the buffalo robes, and certain ones carried the deer hides and other soft skins. They always had tents made out of skin, and before the horses, they carried them.

Nowadays, they have corn soup and fry bread, but in those days our grandmothers would grind corn and mix it with water and then put it between two leaves and that was the bread; they would roast it. Then the dried meat, they would make it into a wasna [pemmican]; it's cherries and dried deer meat together and the marrow of the bone. They had corn and they had beans. The beans were always stored by the river. They were little round ones; they would grind them up and take leaves and put it by the fireside and that would cook. So that's the food that they ate.

Our ancestors didn't have no bowls, pots, and pans, and so when they dried skins they would kind of make them like a bowl and then if it's cold they put it by the fire and they put tea in there. Maybe it would take about four or five hours but that heat would blend it.

The elderly grandmothers always carried a knife, mina, and they had a flint so they were ready to cook. So nowadays you see traditional women [dancers] having a knife at the back.

Whenever our ancestors found some cherries, they would leave some with tobacco, so they would have another food crop next year. Then in the history books it tells that we were horse thieves, but this isn't true; they would have a little tobacco and they would leave it there and then the people that own these horses, they would look for any sign of tobacco and if they see [it], then they'll know that they pay for them horses like that. So that tobacco was always important.

My grandmother used to say that they did not cut any tree; they used only the tree that shed its leaves. They would watch it; if that didn't grow then the husky men would just keep pushing on it till it falls over and then they would take it to the campsite.

They used to use a buffalo robe long time ago when our ancestors died. If anybody was sick and they know they're going to die, well, a grandmother, she'll get sage and sweetgrass; she'll have it in this medicine bundle and then she'll have deerskin, buffalo robes. So when that person left for the spirit world, they would call on her. If it was a man, then she'd get a man to come and help her and they would wash them with sage and they would start wrapping them up with these deerskins and then at last was the buffalo robe.

If you were in mourning, you put all the mourners together in a circle and you give them the sacred pipe, and then they would pray and share that, but only one man touches that pipe, the medicine man.

Our buffalo robes are gone. That's what they used to use going on the hill [on a vision quest]; take a buffalo robe if it's cold; and you could have it for name-giving ceremony and honoring ceremony and marriage ceremony. That was their sina, their blanket; that was their home.

So it was no easy way of life for our ancestors. They had to work what God gave them, preserve it and take care of it. They always fed the water, they would put tobacco in there. I do that yet. I go down to the Missouri River, I pray and I give it tobacco.

Our ancestors wanted to just be free to travel because if you put them on the reservations, they said, "We're gonna starve" and that's what they did; they [the government] rationed food to them. The soldiers were dipping hard-tack in coffee or tea and then eating it in front of our ancestors while they were hungry. They'd eat a piece of meat and instead of giving it to them they'd throw it out to the dogs.

There was no circle of life; it was slowly breaking apart. They were starving because they couldn't go plant corn, and they couldn't go make tea, they couldn't dig up turnips, they couldn't get cherries, they couldn't get anything because if you leave the reservation you get punished and it was always the soldiers that were the killers.

Our ancestors didn't have nobody to run to for help; they went in the four directions but there was nobody there. They couldn't go to the white man; they couldn't go to their ancestors because they killed them off. So then with their pipe this way [pointing toward the sky] they faced the west and our grandmothers sang this song:

Tunkasina, Mahpiya Duta heciya initancan ye
[Grandfather, you are chief there in the Red Sky (Heaven)]
Unci maka kin deciya nankun initancan ye, ye
[Over here on Grandmother Earth, you are also chief]
Taku yakage hena iyuha na wiconi nahan wakan yakage ye
[All those things you made and people's lives, sacred you made them.]
Oyate Duta kin de unkiyepi ye
[These are the Red People]
Oksansan etuwan unkinajin pi ye, ye
[We stand facing all around]
Maka sintomni iyotiyekiya takoza kin ob na'unzin pi ye
[All around the land we stand pitifully with our grandchildren]
Tunkasina, Wakan Tanka, tuweni wacin'unyapi sni ye.
[Grandfather, Great Spirit, we have nobody to depend on.]

The last part is:
Tunkasina, Wakan Tanka, niye, niye, niye,
[Grandfather, Great Spirit, you, you, you,]

Nisnana wacin'uniyapi ye, ye.
[Only you, we depend on you.]
Lilililililililililili!

It means:

> We look in the four directions
> There's nobody there to help us
> We are your Red people
> Don't forget us
> Forgive us our sins whatever we done.
> So we look up to you and
> you're the only one that can help, you.

That's the end. It's a long song but I learned it from my grandmothers.

My teachers were my grandmothers; my mother was too busy with raising seven boys. They taught me how to dry corn, pound cherries, and dry plums, and gather medicine and the wild fruits along the rivers, and they'd take me to the prairie and tell me about the medicines out there.

The plums were big; when they got red, that's when our grandmothers would wash their hands, sage [purify with burning sage] their hands, and then they would take the seed out, line them up, and dry them in the sun. And then when they were all dried, they would pack them in light deerskin, the stomach part, hang it up and then they would sage again.

My grandparents was always tanning hides and it took a long time; they would use brains [from the animal] and I'd sit there and help them. Then they got some white clay and put it on there and rub it some more and if they wanted it smoke colored then a special fire [was] built for that and it would get that smoky colored.

We drank skunk oil for our colds and my grandmother would rub my braids with it, and then early in the morning she'd take me down the river and she'd wash my head off with soap and I would have no skunk smell, nothing. We used to put a little sugar in there and drink it and then we used to eat it too.

The way to skin that skunk is a man has to do that and he's praying, "My kids are hungry, my grandchildren are hungry, they've got to eat. We only want one deer today, we want a couple of buffaloes today; there's young couples going to get married, they need a sina, a robe, and there's going to be babies being born, we've got to have some rabbit skins." That's the way our ancestors prayed.

My grandmothers were really sincere, they always was humble, liked to share. They never asked, "You want a cup of coffee?" They didn't say that. They'd go up and take a cup and they'd put coffee in there; they'd look in their cupboards to see if there's a piece of bread. "Ho, nana yuta," that means, "Here, eat this—be strong." That's the way my grandmothers were.

My grandma she'd be cooking or making bread and she'd tell us that her and her sister and their parents were someplace in South Dakota but they had to go to Minnesota to get wild rice, exchange. Her and her sister were very young, she said, and here these soldiers were coming and all them young girls they were raping them; so her and her sister went and hid in this great big rock and they were saved.

It must have been horrible because my grandmother had tears in her eyes; I'm old now and I'm remembering what they're telling me, and they want to forget, they want to forgive them but they can't forget how they were treated that way, so their eyes get misty.

I never was to the Black Hills when I was growing up. All those sacred sites at the Black Hills was a place to go and worship God. Our ancestors called it "He Sapa". The word "He" means like a deep forest; they sit there and them trees are growing out of the rock, so our ancestors they said, "Wanuktasni"; that means "mystery," wanuktasni wakan—everything was wakan [sacred] because God made that. Our ancestors would sit there and you could hear the spirits talk and you're talking to God but then God doesn't talk to you; He talks to you through the winds. They knew there was gold there; our grandfathers would go hunt in the Black Hills and they would drink water and then they'd tell each other, "Inyan zi," gold; they would hold it for a little while and then they'd put it back.

The white man will never understand how sacred that land is, not only Bear Butte but a lot of other places. They said nobody ever climbed them hills. Our grandfathers did without equipment; they just studied it and prayed and then said, "Hoka"—that means "okay"—and then they climbed them. They climbed the highest one; they [non-Indians] call it Devil's Tower. I hate that name; Paha Wakan is what our ancestors called it, the Sacred Hill, the Sacred Mountain.

These people that go to the Black Hills, they save their money all winter and they go there to enjoy themselves; they're not going to pray.

It makes me feel bad, especially this gambling at Deadwood; it makes me feel sad because that was a place to worship God, to give food to the spirits. There's a lot of sacred things in the Black Hills, but it's not for me to say it because just a little while ago my whole body kind of warmed up and that's all I'm going to say.

My dad worked all the time and my mother was always doing something; if it was the season for fruits and for cherry-picking, or in the springtime she'd gather up the mint and she'd pick out what roots she needs. We lived in a tent for many years and then we lived in a shack, so my parents lived in a shack till they both died. They didn't have no rent to pay, no light bill to pay and the water was free and the turnips and everything that was on Mother Earth.

I grew up the hardship way. There was never no candy, or no apples or oranges, but my grandma always told us to appreciate what God gave us. There's a lot of times I went to bed hungry. On the reservation sometimes Mama would say, "You kids be quiet now, Daddy went to go hunt." But I know that she was praying. 'Cause pretty soon it'll be dark and he brought something back and then they'd be butchering; no matter how late it was she'd cook, she'd wake us up and we'd eat; just meat, just fried meat. Then daddy would always pray, "Thank you God for what you gave us, it sure filled my kids up."

I went to school when I was five years old at Stephan, South Dakota; it was a Catholic mission. I knew how to read and write, and do sewing, and to work mostly, and we sure done a lot of praying! We weren't supposed to pray in our own language; they didn't teach us that, only the white man's language, we're supposed to know that, we're supposed to forget and not be like our ancestors, the "red savages"; we were taught that.

I couldn't understand why they was cutting my hair short; they chopped off our braids and gave us bangs. They thought we was lousy; make us take all our clothes off and put some kind of an ointment on our heads and then they even gave us some ointment to put on our faces—gee it burned our eyes! "Oh," I said, "Somebody help us!" You know, we're screaming but whatever ointment they gave us, [it was] really painful to our eyes and in those days if our ancestors knew what child abuse was they would have got it first degree!

When we got to school they said, "We're going to tell you about God and God's name is Jesus." So they showed us a cross and how He died, He sacrificed for us "pagan heathens." We didn't know what pagan heathens were, we thought they were good names. We got up at six, hurry up, washed our hair, changed our clothes, made our beds and the nun would inspect that. Then we'd go downstairs; we stand in line to go to church at seven. We filed to church, we received communion and we'd come back again. Then we went for breakfast, we prayed, we got through eating, we prayed and when we got to school we prayed. When we got out of school we prayed. We had to pray for the sinners; we had to pray to the saints; we had to pray to Jesus that he would forgive our sins, and we had to pray to ask Jesus to forgive our ancestors for the sins they committed for killing the white man.

They hit us for nothing and they were telling us things that was right only in their way. I don't think they were thinking about God, otherwise they wouldn't be doing that. They should have told us the truth, they lied to us. They said Christopher Columbus found this country. "Oh Christopher Columbus, he just came and he was a saint, he was a holy man," you know. "He came and he educated; he taught your grandparents how to talk the right way and then he brought a cross, Christopher Columbus. He brought a cross and set it there and then from there, 'Thou shalt not kill, thou shalt not steal.'" Christopher Columbus wasn't thinking about God; oh, when he saw this country he must have hollered, "Bingo!" [laughs]

All these things that they were teaching us was wrong. I look at it that way now in my old age; my ancestors weren't no dirty redskins, that's the color that God gave us. Then they said our ancestors never prayed but yet when I'd go home from school, I would see my grandfather praying.

I had two grandpas and two grandmas on each side and then my great-grandparents; they were all pipe carriers. My grandparents talked about the Pipestone quarry, Inyan Sa Makoce; that means "red stone." There was a great flood and the blood kept flowing until it turned into stone. Way before the white man came they went to that place; they circled around and then they took tobacco, cansasa, they prayed. They're going to take just enough [pipestone] to make a family cannunpa [pipe]. They used only their hands and their rocks to chip away enough. Not every person carried a pipe, just one person in that clan, tiospaye. He would have this and then if there was problems like no food or which way we were going to go—"Wace' unkiya pi kte, we have to pray." So they would pray and then they would move on.

I don't know how old I was, maybe about five or six years old, but I remember the sun was just setting down and that grandmother had the pipe; she was praying in Dakota and then she'd touch Mother Earth. Then, I would say, in the thirties, I never did see the sacred pipe. Our ancestors, our grandmothers, our parents, they had to put away their cannunpas, their sacred pipe, and eagle feathers; they couldn't use them no more and if they were brought out they were going to punish them.

My grandfathers, of course, they couldn't use the sacred pipe, so then they'd light up a Bull Durham; "Ho, nis'inya, wasicu, Here, I give you this rolled [white man's tobacco]," and my grandfather would light that and then together they'd just puff, you know, let the smoke out. So my grandfather, his people that come to see him, he blessed them.

My grandmother never went to church, she quit. She stayed home and she'd pray with tobacco. I watched what they were doing; every once in a while they were butchering and they'd throw a piece of meat out. I'd go over there and they'd say [in Dakota] "Leave that meat alone. We fed the spirits."

The pipe started coming back in the seventies since that Freedom of Religion [Act]. We could take out our pipes and pray, we could take out our eagle feathers and pray, we could sage. I'm sixty-six years old and how was I ever going to get involved with my own Indian religion? I didn't look for it; it came to me. One boy he came and he gave me a cannunpa and he told me, "You're going to need this so you use it the right way."

I got the *Lakota Times* and I read in there that there was going to be the Annual Pipe Run to Pipestone that was going to be [led] by Arvol

Looking Horse [Spiritual Leader of the Lakota Nation, and Keeper of the Sacred Calf Pipe, which lies at the core of Lakota spiritual beliefs]. They want to stop the abuse of taking the red rock [pipestone] and just carving anything out of it. . . . My niece [had given] me some earrings, and they were made out of real pipestone. I looked at them for a long time; I couldn't put them on. . . . Harold [Ironshield, one of the run's organizers] came to my house and he was telling me, "You know, there's a lot of Dakotas and Lakotas in this town but nobody's interested."

So I said, "What do you want me to do? How can I help you?"

"Well, I'm trying to get some funds to take out there. They're [the runners] coming by Selby now."

That quick, I got my family, and we made two big plastic jugs full of lemonade, and we took all kinds of food over there to that little park by Selby and sure enough, they were there. I thought that there'd be a lot of Sioux; I just expected cars and cars, and vans. Just pitiful! "Oh gosh," I said, "you mean all the Sioux in this whole state of South Dakota and that's all there is there? I'm getting involved." They were going to be here [in Aberdeen] for four days, so I rented this park and Harold paid for it. They camped and I got the town people here to feed.

Then we went to Toka Bay. I come back and got some more food, and got some more money and went to Brookings. Oh gosh, going out of Brookings we stopped at Blue Cloud Abbey and here they didn't want us there. So we went to that little park by the road and we parked there and we ate supper. Then I said, "You guys, this ain't the only time we slept on the ground." So even me, I slept on the ground and I was laying there looking up at the stars and I was really praying.

The next morning we got to Harmony Hill, another Catholic place. They fed us in the garage! Two days we stayed there, then we went to Lake Poinsett. Oh that lady [in the store] got nasty! "How dare those dirty Redskins," just like that to me and Wayne Red Horse [a runner].

"Come outside and say that," I said.

"I'm protected."

"Who's protecting you?" I said.

"A gun."

"There's somebody more powerful than a gun," I said.

They [non-Indians] don't understand what we're doing. They call us all kinds of names! I always stay behind the runners to see that they're protected. We went to Flandreau and from there we went into Pipestone. There we were on sacred land, our ancestors' blood. When I travel on this pipe run, I take it [her pipe] with me. To be a pipe carrier you've got to be strong, you've got to be brave, you've got to be compassionate to people. You can't lie, oh gosh, and you can't take money. So it's hard to be a pipe carrier.

I met my husband a long time ago. You see his reservation's across the river from mine and so we knew each other when we were really young and then finally, we got married, but we only had one child. We always lived in a log house; I graduated from the tent to the log house. [laughs] We lived mostly on his reservation, Lower Brulé, not in the community but out in the country on his grandparents' land.

We went to wacipi [dances]. I was a traditional dancer. I never danced fancy because my ancestors never danced fancy, just really traditional dancing on Mother Earth. You're not supposed to look around to see if anybody's watching, you're supposed to stand there with the eagle feather, look down, you know, just stand there and pray. Our ancestors they danced when the moon came up. Certain times they had pipe ceremonies; the men danced in a circle and then the women stood on the side and they danced traditional.

When I first got married, every morning I'd make baking powder biscuits, and then dinner I was making them, supper I was making them. Now I can't do that; just to look at that flour and that baking powder I'm tired. [laughs] He [her husband] used to hunt deer and I would dry meat; that's when we depended on Mother Nature to be the ice box. [laughs] We didn't have no electricity, just lamps.

If you wanted to take a bath, I had to haul water from the river and put it in the tubs. In the wintertime that was every other day for me, but the men, they toughed it out clear up until last part of October; they'd go take a dive in the river.

The river water was for washing clothes, blankets, and scrubbing wood floors. If I had to cook, he'd have to go outside and bring in the kindling and get the stove started and then we never had bacon and eggs—who thought of bacon and eggs? But we had oven biscuits and we'd have fried potatoes or oatmeal and then if there was any meat I'd fry it crispy. I guess it [life] was hard, but who was thinking about them hardships? [laughs]

Everybody worked then; you know nowadays the white man says we're "lazy Indians" but we weren't. He [her husband] used to go chop wood and I used to help him. The white ranchers used to ask for cedar poles for fence-making and they'd tell him, "We got to have 400, 500 cedar poles," and he'd come and he'd tell his mother and so all that time [he was working] she'd be saging [burning sage]; she was praying for him. Boy, this bought a lot of groceries!

Then if he wanted any boots, well, then he had to save, save, save. His mother had a lot of lease money so she was always helping out. Whenever I wanted clothes, I'd go back to my reservation and my mother would get lease money and then she'd buy me clothes. Even though I got married, we had to depend on our parents because there was no jobs, nothing.

My dad said, "You better get out of this hell hole." So then I came here [Aberdeen] and I went to work at Saint Luke's Hospital. From there I went back to Sisseton and I worked for that tribe for six years.

My parents they left the reservation too. My mother used to wash dishes in a cafe and my dad would do construction work.

My husband worked on construction here; that's the only thing he could find. He worked different places and he worked in Clark potato fields; he was sorting them, grading them, then they priced them; he'd load them up on that big semi and then they'd go and they'd load the next semi. He done that for a long time, twenty years.

I just sit here and I think back to the reservation; that life down there was a hell. To this day it's worse; there's no hope down there.

Now I make myself strong because I almost died in the University [Hospital in Minneapolis]. My small intestine was wrapped around the big intestine. They took me out of here in an air ambulance. They [her relatives] came and put a eagle feather here [points to chest]. My nephew's a medicine man. He was praying outside of my door. They [the hospital staff] wouldn't allow him to bring that pipe in but the eagle feather they did. I had a funny dream. I seen my ancestors. They didn't talk, they were dark-skinned, long black hair, one had a basket and they was holding things. They never looked at me but silently they were around me. Then I looked to the door and a flash of lightning would come and go, just come and go.

The hardest part that I ever had, the greatest, was six months later. I come out of the hospital. I couldn't walk, I weighed 140 pounds. I looked all around and there's my nephew, his wife, kids, my brother but they're all silent. They didn't say nothing. They were glad to see me but yet I was missing somebody. I said in Sioux, "Eli, tokiya he?" [Where is Eli? (her husband)] Oh gosh, there was more silence. Sister Charles said, "Stella, we buried him."

"Huh?" I said.

"We buried him," and the whole world fell apart. Then I wanted to die.

He would come and see me [in the hospital]. He came one night and they found him five o'clock in the morning. My brother said, "Eli's car is over there; better go tell him to come in." Here he had all the doors locked, the windows rolled up, and on the side there that little window was open. They reached in there and he was bloated. The police drove him down to the hospital and the doctor came and said, "He's died."

Crying, crying, that's all I did was just cry, and I couldn't eat. Then

I had a memorial; I've got to be brave, I've got to thank God. I made star quilts and I thank God for healing me, and I had a memorial for my husband.

Then them bills started coming in and they're going to come and take my car away because I owe two thousand. Things was getting worse, they're going to sue me, they're going to put me in jail. "If I die," I said, "I wouldn't have to pay for these bills." I'd go on the road and see if a semi would come and I was going to hit that semi but you know, I never met no semi.

One night I was driving around and I was looking for a medicine man but I know there's no one around here you can depend on. "I've got to find a Catholic priest," I said. I didn't have no money and I was tired. I just drove and here I seen a light. It was about nine o'clock and I drove in there and I pushed that buzzer and a tall Catholic priest came. "Come on in," he said, "come on in." So I went in. I was going to tell him [about Eli], confess my sins, and then for sure I'm going to kill myself.

The police department have seven pictures of my husband, how he died, you know which way he was laying. So this Catholic priest went there. "I'm concerned for that Indian woman," he said. "You folks found her husband dead in this town and is there anything being done?"

"No, he just died of natural causes." They let him see them pictures and so then that's when he got involved. He went to the BIA, so that's how they paid for my bills. They paid everything, Dr. Najarian, forty-one thousand; Dr. Janus, thirty-six thousand: air ambulance, a thousand five—oh that's a lot of money!

Then I had a dream. I think my husband knew that I was crying for him. We had an old car; it was a black four-door Ford 1947. I could see this black car going skyward and he was waving, he was really waving. My husband's gone to the spirit world. I thought him and I would grow old together, and we'd watch our grandchildren, and it didn't happen that way.

I got his axes in there; this summer I'm going home to the reservation so I'm going to have my brother dig a hole and I'm going to bury them. Nobody will ever use them.

For me to be a grandma nowadays I have to have money; quarters, pennies, they don't count; they want dollars now because you can't get anything for a quarter no more. So I try to teach my grandchildren to do something before they get paid: sweep the floor, empty the garbage. I'm teaching them how to work, how to say pidamayaye [thank-you], and how to pray, and to ask the grandma, "Do you want a cup of water? You want me to do something?" All this is important.

It's hard because they don't want to listen to you, they don't want to learn anything; that's the sad part for me, they're not paying attention, they're not watching me. After I'm gone they'll say, "Remember, grandma used to be drying corn and pound cherries and dry them? Well then, it's our turn."

Long time ago corn was the main source of food. They would grind it up and make corn-balls. You go out and you get it at the right time; it can't be too young. When it's yellow, that's when you have a ceremony. [She dries corn as she talks.] I prayed here and I said, "The food that you brought to our ancestors, that you gave to us to use, now I will be feeding the people. There's some people that are going to be hungry, and there's going to be visitors coming, so bless this corn, and bless the corn that's out there."

And then I cook it for fifteen minutes, I don't time it—I ain't got time for that! I just come sit here and cut diamonds and I'm over there trimming my star quilts and then it's time to take it out. After all that then it takes two, three days for it to cool, then it gets hard, and then you could husk [shuck] them.

If I go home to my reservation, I already got a big long table down there, so all I got to do is just husk them here and then take them down there. By that time they'll be ready to go, it all depends on [whether] God gives me sunshine. We have to choose a sunny day, so that takes almost twenty-four hours to take care of; the wind and the sun dry it. It's really got to be dry before you put it away. So that's how I made mine. If that was on a reservation I'd finish it maybe in three weeks but here in town it takes longer, almost a month and a half. On the reservation it's easier because there you got all kinds of help.

There used to be a lot of us grandchildren. Our grandmother used to make us wash our hands and then she would sage her food. There was no screen or anything to protect the corn from the flies so all day we used to swat them flies with tree branches. Now, I don't know who's going to do this.

I'm getting to the point where I have to make plans because I keep telling God, I said, "You know when you're going to come but I don't know." So I have to be prepared. Nowadays it's hard; our grandmothers they didn't want nobody to have hardship so when it's time for them to die—they didn't know but they were getting close to it—they would make themselves beautiful moccasins and dresses and shawls so they were getting ready.

I have no daughter to give my shawls away. My nieces they don't know how to sew, but in time when I'm gone, well then they'll put these star blankets together, and they'll pound cherries, they'll dry corn, but right now they have to work and support their families.

My oldest granddaughter is in Sioux Falls; she's over there to the white man's world but she'll remember that I was a Dakota, I'm a Red woman, I'm a Red grandma, and she'll say, "Well, Grandma wasn't mean, she was always giving, so it's our turn." They can't make these [star quilts] but they could have giveaways, so I'm telling them, "When I die you feed the people and give away all my shawls, all my blankets, all my property." I said, "That same day in the evening feed the people, have a giveaway. Don't have no memorial for me because you girls are having a hard time." But at the end they won't listen to me they'll have it anyway. [laughs]

I'm all alone in my house but then I pray a lot and I have the sacred pipe and I have prayer book and I have the rosary because I believe in these; I pray with them, so God hears my prayers. There's nobody here to tell me anything about traditional. There's nobody here to tell me about the sacred pipe, the cannunpa. No matter if I went to white-man's school all my life—I was taught to pray in the white man's way—yet I can't forget my language. I pray like my ancestors did; they would look up to thank God for the stars and the moon and especially Mother Earth, and thank God for the water and the medicine and the food that grows. He took care of us; He didn't let us down. Now that there are these dams and chemicals, it's all gone; you almost have to find a secret place to find fruit or else you have to pay somebody to get you some, and then that person has a secret place.

I don't have nothing myself but I always manage to make soup and fry bread and if I know somebody's hungry, well I just go and I pass it out and I gather up clothes and I go just give 'em away.

I'm old and before I die I wish there would be peace. When Tunkasina Wakan Tanka made us, he gave us these four colors, the black, the yellow, the red, and the white.

I always used to have hate for the white man because they done so much killing. The white man tried to kill our ancestors, to make us extinct, you know, just fade away, but we're still here. We have to forgive each other and we have to shake hands and be friends. So I'm talking peace now; I can't have hate for anybody in my heart.

Our greatest enemy right now is alcohol and drugs and it's a silent massacre. Our grandchildren are getting weak. There's no hope; they want to die. Our grandchildren are dying by the hundreds. They are dying on the road and killing themselves; they pull a trigger and blow their brains out. They use alcohol more and commit crimes; the penitentiary is filled with the grandchildren. That's not the way. So this alcohol has taken a lot of lives. That's the only sadness I have. My hopes and dreams is that some day this alcohol and drugs will leave all the reservations.

So I do a lot of praying nowadays. I live for that—to get up in the morning and pray my Sioux way because I'm supposed to pray that way. I said, "I could be in church but I'm a Dakota; my house is a church, outside, these hills and mountains and every place where we worship you and we pray to you and give thanks and honor you and call you by your Indian name, that's our church."

And I thank God, I said, "Tunkasina Wakan Tanka, anpetu wan waste unyak'u pi.... You gave us a good day to honor you, to give you thanks that there's no bombs up in the air, there's no machine guns pointing at us, they're not using chemicals on us; you are watching out for us so we thank you for our lives because you're the head of it. So thank you for Mother Earth; the white man calls it the United States of America." Then I ain't got time to be sad. I gotta go. [laughs]

Cecilia Hernandez Montgomery

CECILIA HERNANDEZ MONTGOMERY, *an Oglala Lakota, grew up on the Pine Ridge Reservation. She has lived in Rapid City since 1945. Now in her eighties, she has been a community organizer for almost fifty years and continues to be actively involved in numerous committees serving the native community. She still finds time to pass on Lakota stories and traditions to her grandchildren and when she speaks to elementary-school classes.*

I'm Cecilia Hernandez Montgomery and I was born on the Pine Ridge Reservation back on November 2, 1910, and my hometown is Kyle, South Dakota. I was born and brought up out in the country. I come from a big family and I'm the oldest. I had four brothers and five sisters.

My parents were hard-working people. My dad was a good cattle-man and that's how he raised his family. I think he learned that from his own dad because my grandfather, after he settled down, he raised a lot of cattle, and it went on to the next generation. My dad was a good provider. My mother raised a garden and did a lot of canning, and naturally, we all worked together as a family.

When we were kids we used to do a lot of riding because we had to herd cattle, and we had to bring the milk cows in. Me and my brothers and my sisters used to milk cows; we had thirteen cows and we each milk two. Many is the time I got kicked over by a cow, my milk bucket and all. [laughs] Oh, those were the good old days!

All the boys used to have to help my dad in the spring of the year when the cows were calving. One time they brought back a half-frozen calf, and brought it into the kitchen. We all sat up and nursed it all night giving it milk so it'll survive.

Everything came from the garden; eggs came from the chickens and our meat, milk, and butter came from our cows. My grandpa on my mother's side, he was a hog raiser. Every time they butchered over there, he used to bring my mother maybe half a hog, and they'd make their own bacon. My mother used to dry meat, make this jerky—you know how they used to dry meat in the olden days. They had these root cellars that they dug in the ground and so my mother used to put all her canned stuff down there and even hang her meat in there. My dad used to ship cream to Rapid City and every week when the check come, he used to divide it among us kids for milking the cows and running the separator, and that's how we earned our cash.

We used to get out in the potato field because potato bugs were so thick on the leaves, and if we didn't pick them, they'd kill the plants. In the fall of the year we had to shuck corn, pick potatoes, and gather carrots and turnips. We were brought up the hard way but we never did go hungry.

We didn't have electric lights. We used kerosene lamps and we used a wood stove. There was a lot of laundry to be done and we used to wash this all by hand with those great big old-time washboards. I'll never forget that cause my brothers used to have big overalls and we used to have overalls galore to wash and we'd fill that whole line. Oh, I dreaded wash days!

We never went to no big cities. The only big town we knew was Gordon, Nebraska, because after we got big and the kids went to school, I remember we used to go pick potatoes in the potato fields in Nebraska, and that's how we earned our winter money and then after potato picking, my dad would bring us back to school. [laughs]

I think my whole family went to Catholic mission school at Holy Rosary Mission, Pine Ridge, South Dakota, 'cause we were strictly a Catholic family and my parents saw to it that we got a good Catholic education. Well, back in them days the government schools were sort of run like military, but we weren't. It was strictly Catholic. It was run by priests and nuns and brothers. A lot of them came over from Germany. It was a boarding school, and they must have carried about 500 students in them days. Of course, the girls had their own dorms and the boys had their own dorms and we were kept separate, like the boys had their own classroom and we had ours, and the same way with the dining room. And when we went to church the boys all knelt certain pews over here and the girls that side.

I was raised up very strict where I didn't have a boyfriend till I was fifteen years old, didn't even know what a boyfriend was—you know how it is when you go to a Catholic school! The only time we had recreation was special occasions. We used to have picnics in the spring of the year, and that's when all of the kids would get together. They had a big beautiful picnic grounds in the trees and whenever we went to that picnic grounds, we had brothers and nuns stationed all over keeping a really close watch on us. We couldn't even sit close together when we visited, or hold hands but we used to sneak and hold hands. [laughs]

When we had entertainments like Christmas dance or something, we had to hold each other mile long and dance around. [laughs] I remember my boyfriend he said, "Let's hold close together, see what happens." So I was holding him close and pretty soon one of the nuns came along and kind of parted us. I knew that was going to happen, but we just wanted to see what would happen. [laughs] I tell you, bring you up in a Catholic school, you just have to toe the mark.

We had plenty to eat because they raised their own cattle, their own hogs, their own chickens. I remember we used to have to clean chickens, and I didn't like the smell of feathers. They had big gardens, and this brother used to make his own sauerkraut down in the basement, barrels and barrels of sauerkraut and barrels of dill pickles too! If you got a chance to work in the kitchen, then we used to sneak down into the basement and steal dill pickles. [laughs] Oh, that was funny! "Who was down in the basement?" you know, the sister couldn't help but smell that dill pickle when she'd come back!

We used to have to slice meat by hand, and we used to sneak some of it between bread and stick it in our pockets and snack on it. [laughs] When you're young you do a lot of crazy little things.

My parents took us to school in September and we never got out of there until about June first. We stayed there nine months out of the year and we never did get to go home, so our parents used to come and visit us on special occasions. They had a regular campground there, so they would bring their tents and camp. In them days they had to travel by horse and wagon. See, this was back in the twenties. That's why I always say I'm from the roaring twenties and the dirty thirties. [laughs]

They used to come for Christmas and they would let us go and visit them, and oh, my mother would cook up a big storm for us. We'd get hungry for home-cooked food; she'd make us wojapi [berry pudding], and fry bread, and bring papa saka [beef jerky], and cook everything that we liked that we didn't get at the school, so we used to be tickled when they'd come and camp.

At Easter time they'd come again; that would be in the spring of the year and she'd bring eggs and things and we used to sit out there in the tent and help her dye eggs. [laughs] I used to enjoy that because we never see them months at a time. My dad was a Catholic catechist, so he used to come to Holy Rosary occasionally to get his instructions from the priest that he worked with and he would come and visit us; but other than that we don't get to go home.

Of course at vacation time everybody used to come after their children in wagons and they'd bring horses for the boys to ride home. We lived, I would say, fifty miles from Kyle to Holy Rosary; they used to come and take the cut-across roads. One time my dad drove the wagon and my mother drove the buggy and they had brought two saddle horses along for my two brothers to ride home because we were a big family. My sister Alice and I drove the buggy home and my dad, my mother, and the little ones took that big wagon, and my two older brothers rode the horses. So those were the good old days!

I graduated from there in the eighth grade and then I went back the following year for the ninth grade. I took music for eight years when I was going to school there. My parents paid $15 or $20 a year for music lessons. So I tell you, I got music in my brains till the day I die. I'll never forget the notes cause every time you made a little mistake on the piano or the organ, this teacher would be sitting there and she had a long ruler, and boy, she'd whack our hands! I sure learned music the hard way, I got it knocked into me. [laughs]

I learned to play the church organ; I love to play music and I love to sing but in my old age my voice ain't what it used to be anymore. After I left Holy Rosary I went to Genoa Indian School. In the school orchestra I played the C-melody sax and I played the piano, so I think wherever I went I carried music with me. Music meant more to me than my educational needs because after I went to Genoa we took geometry and I just couldn't make heads or tails out of it for a long time. I finally did catch on but I never did get no good grades. Eventually I did finish my schooling and I met my husband while I was going to school there.

The funny part of how I met him was he was an all-around athlete. He was very popular with the high school boys and he was captain of the basketball team and he was captain of the football and a group of us girls we were cheerleaders. It was four of us used to stand out in the front and lead the rest, and here, I guess at one of these football games, he said, "Who's that big-mouth cheerleader? I want to meet her after the game." [laughs] That was me and that's how I met him.

So what happened next was he invited me to the banquet. In them days we had a grand march right up to the banquet and I was his partner and after that we got, you know, closely related and that's how we wound up getting married. He finished high school in '32 but I didn't get to finish my high school. I finished eleventh grade and I got married that year.

I don't know too much about my grandparents on my dad's side because it seems to me they passed away when I was still a child. On my mother's side I knew them real well. His name was Alexis Mousseaux, Tahanpa Sapa [Black Moccasin], and he was a French-born Canadian, my grandfather. He came from Fort Robinson with the cavalry when that Wounded Knee Battle was going on; my grandfather was Indian scout. They tried to work with the soldiers, the Indian scouts, but I guess they wouldn't listen to them. He did get to see so much of that shooting and killing and how the Indians were just shot down in their tents and lot of them froze to death because that happened in wintertime.

His wife was one of the Wounded Knee victims; she didn't die but she was shot in her hip and in her leg and in her arm. So she was partially paralyzed from there; she walked on her leg but it was crooked, that was how it was healed. In them days they didn't have doctors.

I think they called her Foolish Woman, that was her Indian name;

but that was one of my grandpa's first wives. I never knew this grandma that was in Wounded Knee because she died. The second wife that he had is the one that bore him lot of children and her name was Wagmu Su, that means "Pumpkinseed," and they had ten children, eight daughters and two sons. That's where my mother came from and that's where I originated from.

But on my father's side, my grandfather is one of these Mexicans that came over from Mexico during the cattle drives they had back in the 1800s. He was a Mexican cowboy and he drove cattle from Texas into the northern states for some big company they called Seven L Cattle Company. His name was Manuel Hernandez. He married a fullblood Indian woman. Her Indian name was He Sapa, Black Horn, and there was five boys and three girls from that family. My dad's name was Ambrose; he was the oldest one, and then there was one named Florencio, and then Valentino and Reyes and Catalina and Anastasia and Rosita. So I got Mexican blood in me. When my grandparents were together that's all they talked but after that us kids never did know the lingo because my dad never did talk it.

I used to have a grandma on my dad's side that was in Wounded Knee. That was my dad's aunt from his side of the family. We called her Lame Grandma and her leg was shattered and it was never set; that leg was just like a child's leg hanging there all her life so she walked on homemade willow crutches. She was a medicine woman—this is what I was coming to.

Her Indian beliefs were strong, her medicine was good; she believed in all the herbs and roots and leaves and she used to come see my mother every now and then. She used to give her, they call them pejuta opahte, that's "medicine bag." She used to bring her these Bull Durham sacks; she used to take those and bring a little bit of everything to my mother and tell her what each one was. That was good medicine, good leaves or herbs or some of it was ground real fine, some of it was put in little packages with little bone grease in it, where they used it for sores and things like that. That's how they used to doctor their own people in the olden days.

She was a good medicine woman; everybody knew her so they always used to rely on Lame Grandma. Her medicine was good, it was the real stuff. She lived to be in her nineties and she died. Just think, I called her the Little Apostle on Crutches.

That's how I learned a lot about roots and leaves and different kinds of flowers that are medicine too. You know this sage that grows wild, that's a medicine and also you burn it and it lets out a good smell and that's supposed to help keep the evil spirits away; same way with the cedar. If you believe in Indian culture, you learn a lot about that so I was telling them kids about it and I think every one of them, when they see sage out there, they say, "Grandma, there's a lot of sage, do you want some?" [laughs] So we usually go and collect sage; sage is sacred to the Indian.

On my father's side we were never that traditional, but my mother's folks were traditional because they were fullbloods on my grandma's side. They call each other the Indian way; that was very respectful in the olden days. My mother, she would call her mother "Ina." Ina means "mother" in Indian. You never call your brothers or sisters by name.

Like an older sister is "cuwe," and a younger sister is "mitankala," and a younger brother is "misun." So I'd address my grandpa, I'd say, "Tunkasila," and my grandmother would be "unci," my mother would be "ina," my dad would be "ate."

Of course in my generation it was different. My mother used to say, "Don't call your brother Joe, call him 'tiblo.'" Anyway, she couldn't get us into that habit, we were so used to talking in English. Like a mother-in-law would never talk to a son-in-law, would never address him, or even sit by him. That's how strict the traditions used to be. Now there are so many changes; I had my son-in-law drive me to town one day. [laughs] He kind of laughed and he said, "You know, if my grandma were living and saw me driving you to town she'd really give us hell." That's why I think all the old Indian traditions are dying off. Look at this young generation; my grandchildren can't even speak Indian, they don't understand Indian. All they know is the English language so I'm afraid that eventually this will all die off; the only thing they'll know is that they're Indian. [laughs]

I remember all the different Indian celebrations that we used to go to in the horse-and-buggy days like Fourth of July. They used to start their Fourth of July celebration with a big morning charge, men, women, girls; the men used to ride bareback on the horse and they carried their guns and bows and arrows. They start before the sun up. They start singing and they start from a certain place where somebody shoots guns and then all the others have to follow but the guns or the arrows they shoot has to go up in the air. I remember we used to be half sleeping and we'd wake up and stand out there and watch them. That used to be really exciting because sometimes there'd be as many as fifty riders that early in the morning. [laughs]

My grandma on my mother's side used to always have one of us carry on some kind of traditional celebration at one of these doings. My brother had maza sala [red penny, or give-away ceremony] one year so they had three tipis set up, they had a big giveaway, and he had to ride a horse. He had three horses that he was leading and every one of them had all kind of Indian stuff on it like beadwork—just think in them days beadwork was just given away, it wasn't sold and it was made by real Indians, blankets and everything. I always remember that.

All that died with our elderly traditional people; you don't see that no more, and that's sad because won't that be great if this generation could see something like that? You know it makes me lonesome, it really does. I always think, "Why couldn't my mother have carried on something like this?" All my grandfolks were just so traditional and it makes me feel so bad when I think of the times that we enjoyed going to those places. [cries]

The other thing that I remember is my sister Alice; the same grandparents picked her to be wiped by a buffalo. The reason they did that was because the Indians believed that when a girl first gets her period that it's sacred; that she's turning into womanhood and that you have to give your blessings to her so that she'll have children. They call it "Tatanka Pakintapi"; that means a buffalo has to come and they do the traditional holy things around you, and they did that to my sister at this celebration.

They had a big tipi and they took her in there and I was curious;

they want just the medicine man and my mother and dad, my grandpa and them. I was asking my aunt, "What are they going to do to her?" and she said, "This buffalo man's going to wipe her with his horns." He's got to be a medicine man that does that; he had a buffalo robe on and buffalo head. She was scared the whole time; she was jerking away trying to get away from him. [laughs] He went in and they were in there for a long time and pretty soon they all come out singing. They say that's a sacred celebration and in the future she would be well and have a family and be strong.

The traditions that they have today have come out from the people that were still traditional and tried to carry it on but it's not like the olden days. Even the sundance ain't what it used to be. Like the sundance in the olden days—I seen it as a teenager—I think three days they have to fast before they go into the sundance and nobody can talk to them. They kept them separate in the tents, and they start early in the morning as soon as the sun peeps out. They don't do that anymore. I think nowadays the sundance is a mockery. The present generation do not realize that this is sacred. They're just doing it for their own good and then they brag about it. They say, "I sundanced. Did you see me out there? I danced and there's nothing to it."

That burns me up, it really does! [sobbing] Things like that really hurt because I've seen it in the olden days where these people danced, even old ones, they danced till they dropped, and you know that the spirit has reached them. But those things are dead.

Another thing that's happening today is these Indian powwows. The present generation just use it as a show to make money for themselves. That is not right and that's not the Indian way. A lot of our elderly say that. Like I said, our forefathers, our grandmothers, when they died they took their traditions with them.

My husband was a Crow Indian from Montana. We got married in 1932 and moved back to the reservation. We settled down at home and he learned how to work with my brothers doing ranch work. My mother passed away in 1939 and that seemed to change all our lives because we were a family that was brought up so closely together that we all lived at home even after we got married. This is what the Indians call "tiospaye," you know the family that's always together. After she passed away we knew that we had to get out on our own and that was hard to do.

We found jobs in Nebraska. The town of Gordon was small at that time but they were really what you call racist. We were going to go in and eat in a little cafe, and here it had a big sign on there said "No Indians Allowed." I remember John, he said, "They're not going to tell me no Indians allowed because I'm going inside anyway." He went in and so the rest of us followed and we all sat down. Everybody looked at us just funny and so this waitress came over and she said, "Haven't you noticed the sign outside the door?" and John said, "No I didn't and if I did I don't care."

She said, "Well, won't you kindly leave or I'll call the police." I'll never forget that and so then my husband said, "You're going to have to throw me out." So we just sat there and pretty soon the manager came over and he said, "Where are you people from?" "We live here in Gordon." He said, "What are your names?" He questioned us a lot so

John turned and said, "My name is John Montgomery, this is my wife, this is my brother-in-law, Joe Hernandez, his wife . . ." and he went on down the line. He looked at all of us and he said, "Well, I'll tell you what, we usually don't serve Indians but you don't look like the type of Indians that cause a lot of trouble." I said, "You know what? We're working people." They had a big place in Gordon where they used to kill turkeys and chickens and they feathered them and we used to do it all by hand; we worked there many years off and on. We told this guy that and believe it or not he let us eat there! You have to know how to defend your rights you know, and after that we never did go back there.

That's what happened in all those Nebraska towns but then of course after we came to Rapid City the same thing happened here. They had signs, "No Indians Allowed." I was surprised to see that even in bathrooms and so there was a lot of discrimination in them days.

We moved to Rapid City in 1945, after my husband got discharged from the service, and we've been here ever since. I went job hunting; a person had to have something to live on because I wasn't on welfare, I didn't know what welfare was about in them days. I always remember I even went to Alex Johnson's Hotel; they needed a dishwasher so I went over and here that lady looked at me and she said, "What did you say your name was?" I said, "Montgomery." She said, "I'm sorry, we don't hire Indians," and that was my first taste then, my first experience.

I found out through my sister that they needed a dishwasher at the A & F Cafe. The guy that owned A & F Cafe owned the Virginia Cafe too and she was working at the Virginia Cafe so that's how I got the job. Some people they'd hire you but some people wouldn't hire you.

Something else I found out years later was about renting. One time I went looking for a house and I gave them my name and when I showed up they found out I was Indian. They said, "Sorry, it's been rented out," but you know they're lying because you know Montgomery sounds reasonable, it's not an Indian name, but if I show my Indian face, then that's it! That was one experience I had.

In some areas here in Rapid City, it's still happening to a lot of our Indians, so discrimination is still around regardless. You can't tell me that everybody's got a heart for an Indian. I guess that these are some of the things that you learn after you get out into the open community and have to make your life in the outside world. You have to find your way around as best you can if you're going to live in a white society. I lived here long enough to understand my white brothers and sisters. We're both human regardless of what color we are; we have to learn to get along.

My husband worked in one of the lumberyards. He started as day laborer and then eventually he worked as a truck driver. John worked for different companies in Rapid City, and I stayed mostly with the cafes. I worked for $3.50 a day washing dishes. I worked myself up into the salad lady's job and then I worked myself into a breakfast cook; pretty soon I was an all-around cook. I worked there for sixteen years at the A & F Cafe. Then they closed the cafe down and they transferred us to another place they call Houk's Drive In. I worked there another six years, then I got sick cause lifting pots was too heavy for me and I had to quit my job as cook.

In between all my work, I was involved in different community activities. Back in the summer of 1968 I was a board member of the Community Action Program (CAP). We started a lot of programs and one of them was a soup kitchen for the low-income elderly. I was in favor of it because we had a lot of our Indian elderly transits that come to Rapid City and they don't have no place to go to eat. So CAP started this program and they asked me if I was interested in being a cook.

They took me off the board and they put me on as the overseer of the soup kitchen. Of course we had to start with donations. I'd do the cooking and I had to have volunteers to help me prepare the meals and serve the elderly. We invited everybody and anybody that was elderly regardless of race, color, or creed, to come and eat.

Then the flood came along in '72 and all that went down with the flood. I didn't work for CAP after that. During the flood they needed volunteers to work with the flood victims, so that's what I did. That was quite a disaster; there was about 126 people that died in the flood and most of them were Indians because they lived along Rapid Creek down on New York and Chicago Streets. A lot of our elderly were lost in the flood because they didn't want to leave their homes; they didn't want to leave what they had. They thought, "Oh, that water won't come this far." We had floods before but it never got to where it was a big disaster. What caused it was the Canyon Lake Dam broke.

The Urban Renewal Program came in and they had in the paper where they needed workers. The unemployment office knew that I was looking for a job, so they told me to go down and put in an application. I said, "I never did do this kind of work. Since I came to Rapid City, I've always been working in kitchens and so forth."

They said, "C'mon Cecilia, you'll get that job because you'll fit in. You know the city well and you're well known in the community." So I applied for the job, and believe it or not, I got it!

I worked for Urban Renewal as a relocation counselor and my job was to place flood victims; we had to find homes for them. A lot of these slum landlords fixed up their places in a hurry so they could rent to the flood victims so we'd have to go to these houses and find out if they were suitable to live in.

We'd put somebody in there and then they'd start having bathroom problems, the water was leaking and different things. I got into it several times with some of those landlords because I wasn't going to keep my people in something like that; so I'd go right back and report it to the city inspector and he'd come out and of course they'd have to fix it up. That would get them so mad! [laughs] I worked for Urban Renewal for five years and then they retired me because I turned sixty-five.

So after that, I didn't work for about a year, and then in '78 I went to work for the South Dakota Green Thumb Program and I worked there for eight years as a field worker. We had to hire elderly on this Green Thumb Program and I think that's when I got concerned about what the elderly needs were because I found out that a lot of our elderly that were able to work yet at fifty-five were not even trying to find a job. They just sit at home and wonder what they're going to do with themselves and I think they deteriorate their lives by not going out and being active. That's one of the things I did since I came to Rapid City, I always kept on the move and kept working. If I ran out of one job I'd look for another and I was pretty well known in the community.

When we first came to Rapid City we stayed with my sister above the railroad tracks on North Maple Street. I used to rent here and there; rent wasn't high in them days but a lot of the slum landlords, they rent to the poor people for little money and the houses weren't too good to live in. So then what we did was we bought our own house for $500 and had it moved down on Oshkosh Street, Twelfth and Omaha. My husband bought it from the airbase; they used it as an office I guess. We divided it into three rooms after we got it. We had to pay lot rent to the owner and we must have lived there for about three years.

All the different Indian people that came into town lived on Oshkosh Street; they called it Oshkosh Indian Camp. This happened in the early thirties and the forties. The Indians had migrated over here and they got jobs with this Warren Lamb Lumber Company. He furnished them houses so there used to be ten houses in that area but they didn't have running water and no indoor toilets. Eventually he hired more Indians and all the people he hired they just camped because they couldn't afford to rent anywhere; he paid them very little wages. They were living in tents and some people bought shacks and moved them down there; it was a regular little reservation. They had outdoor toilets and everybody had to use the same water hydrant. After a while, the white people complained that it was an eyesore.

So that's when the city council decided that Warren Lamb had to improve his houses. So one day they told this Mr. Lamb that he had to modernize his houses or they was going to condemn them. I guess that went on for two or three years but Mr. Lamb never did. They said it was going to cost him too much to remodel those ten houses. One day the city came along and condemned the whole area and they said that they had to get rid of all the Indians that were living there in tents. So then a lot of the Indians moved back to the reservation 'cause they couldn't afford no rent in the city and the ones that did stay, they had to find other places to live.

By that time the Mayor's Committee on Human Relations was formed and they bought twenty acres of land up north. They divided it into lots and at that time these lots were $150 a lot, so my husband and I bought two. We had a little shack so we moved it out here in '52. There was nothing over here. This was like a big, old prairie-dog town. It was dangerous because we ran into a lot of snakes and there was a lot of mice but we had to move someplace. Pretty soon there was others moved out here but they didn't have no houses so they brought their tents and pitched their tents and some of them brought their little shacks. They called us Sioux Addition.

We had to haul our own water from the city hydrant on Fifth Street in them big ten-gallon milk cans, or plastic containers, or whatever containers you have, and that's how we used to take our baths and everything. We had to use wood stoves to keep warm in winter, to cook on and we used kerosene lamps. We still had to use outdoor privies and I tell you it was just like we were living back on the reservation again because we were way out of the city limits. [laughs]

But for seventeen years we hauled water from the city; that's how long we lived out here without water, without heat. Finally there was so much complaints from the school system about our children not having clean clothes to go to school in. Lot of the kids, I guess, didn't look presentable; some of them might not have had their bath, 'cause, see, we were without water. Anyway, the school system started complaining so that's when the Public Health stepped in.

By that time there was more people but they got rid of all the tents and they lived in houses. Of course we had our Sioux Addition Board going then so we were all active and we formed a Sanitary District through the Public Health. The Public Health and the Indian Health decided to get a grant to help the people so they could modernize the houses.

The city had a policy that they don't wheel water to nobody outside of the city limits. We had a lot of support from church groups, the school system, and different groups that said we need water because of the health hazards. So the city had to finally jar loose and break their policy to let us have water. We really put up a fight that time. We even went to City Hall, a bunch of us from here and a lot of the Indians from town too, and when they agreed to give us water everybody yelled and I hollered "Lilililili-lilililili." I really let out my Indian trill and everybody sure liked it, 'cause I was chairman of the Sanitary District. I was so happy I got up and made a big speech. Anyway, I was noted for my big mouth, I guess, for wherever there was something going and if it concerned us, our community, or our Indians, well, I was right there. [laughs]

Sioux Addition has come a long ways. I think we're one of the oldest organizations in Rapid City. I'm proud to say that we are an active group, that we are involved; a lot of us belong to different Indian organizations in Rapid City and we are well known.

That's how we got the Community Action Program out here because we had to go knocking from door to door to see if they would accept this program in the city because it was a poor people's program. I was one of the ones that went knocking from door to door uptown in the city, and many times I got the door slammed in my face because they wouldn't listen to a Indian—let's put it that way—I was Indian and I was asking somebody to help support this program. "We don't need any more Indians in town." That's what some of them told me, so I said, "It's not only for Indians, it's for poor white people too." After a while I got sassy, you know, I had to put it through to them somehow that they could understand but that's when I learned to speak out.

I got interested in different meetings that were going on so I just used to go sit in on their meetings and pretty soon I'd get involved and be part of it. I got involved with the elderly when I was with the National Indian Council on Aging which has an office in Albuquerque. My husband passed away in 1977. He had a heart attack. I had just come back from one of my travels when I heard he was in the hospital, but he passed away before I got to see him. That was a shock! It was hard to take because I was left all alone.

Then I got involved with the White House Council on Aging through the state, and I even got on the South Dakota Governor's Council on Aging. I represented the Indians from the urban areas. To this day I'm still involved in a lot of different community organizations and their meetings.

Right now we have an elderly group, Wawokiye Ospaye—that means "working together" or "helping one another"—and I'm the chairman. We've been going since '85. There was only about four of us and then it gradually got to the point where there's about twenty-three of us now. We work as an advocacy for the elderly.

A lot of our elderly reservation people that come to Rapid City have a hard time relocating and adjusting to the city life, and they don't know where to go, who to turn to, and a lot of them are afraid to ask questions. That's one thing about us Indian people, we're not what you call socially inclined to talk to just anybody. You have to know people so that they understand you and then you can let it all out after you know them, and that's what's happening with a lot of our elderly Indians. We try to get them to dinners and things and explain our programs and what's going on because there's so many needs for the elderly that a lot of our grassroots elderly don't know nothing about. Especially the ones that speak Lakota; they don't understand the big words that they use in a lot of this white language and we explain it to them.

So they call us the Indian Elderly Task Force. Our number one priority is our elderly Indian health. When somebody is in the Sioux San[itarium] Hospital, any of our elderly we know are not getting the right care, we go there and check on them and that's where we went Friday, three of us from our task force. Here there was three elderly up there and this lady was one of them. She was in a car accident, got a whiplash and she broke her wrist.

We got a message that she wasn't getting good care at the Sioux San. We went up there and boy, we shook up that place! We wanted to talk to the head doctor, Doctor Larsen. We wanted to talk to him and they said, "He's busy, he won't be able to see you." "Well, we're going to sit here until we get to see him." And we did! We came in at 10:30, we never got out of there until 4:00. And we finally got them to move this lady to the regional hospital; but Dr. Larsen came and he was in a hurry and he left and he never did come back after that. He knew we were after his ass! [laughs]

Before they turned it into Sioux San, that used to be Rapid City Indian School. After the Indian school closed they turned it into Sioux Sanitarium and for many years it was open to all Indians in the United States that had TB. It's not a sanitarium any more. The Indians in Rapid City needed health care. They couldn't afford to go to the General Hospital. Finally, Sioux San was turned into a hospital for the Rapid City Indians.

So we're going to go every week to visit the hospital because we've had so many complaints from our elderly. Then they tell about some of our nursing homes where our Indian elderly are. They're not being treated right either. So we're going to have to go nosey around them nursing homes and find out what's really going on.

So these are some of the things that's happening to our elderly but we finally woke up to the fact that we have to stand up for ourselves, 'cause nobody else is going to do it; we have to be heard! So we said, "We're going to make it our business. Every time we hear some of our elderly at the Sioux San, we're going to go over there and nosey around and we want something done about it." If the Health Board can't do anything, or if the SUD [hospital administrator] don't try to do something about it, then we're going to go to Doctor Sloan in Aberdeen. If he don't do something about it, we're going to go into Washington. See, we're going to go the route till we know something is done.

So those are some of the things that we see going on with our elderly; health is one of them and housing—those are most important. The others would be transportation and meals. We do have meals programs for the elderly. We have a committee that issues meal tickets to our low-income elderly. Like if I was going to pay for my meal I just couldn't go every day because you have to pay something like a dollar and a half a meal. The meals are cooked in one kitchen down on Fifth Street and from there it's catered to all the other areas.

At Minneluzahan, that's an elderly center, we have a lot of people that come from the west side of town and the south side of town. They are well off, what you call the middle class that can afford it, so they pay cash. We don't have too many Indians that go there to the Minneluzahan, that's a white group. Of course it's open to all the elderly but a lot of our Indians don't like to go there because there's a lot of—they call them "wasicuns" [whites]—and they feel out of place. A lot of the Indians go up to Mother Butler Center because that's more the Indian community north of town.

A lot of landlords are still very racist in who they select to go into their houses. What they do is they rent to our elderly but they give them the lowest kind of housing. We hear about it and we have to bring it up to the Mayor's Needs Assessment Committee. I'll give you an example. This woman, the house she was living in wasn't the best housing but the reason she moved out of there was because the landlord was giving her a bad time because too many of her relatives moved in on her. You know how that goes! She rented that house for her and her daughter, and a grandson but other relatives moved in. The landlord told her that she had to get rid of these people, either that or he was going to raise her rent. She wasn't getting that much money; she was getting ssi and widow's pension but that wasn't much.

South Dakota Adult Services referred her to our program. We visited her house and here her house was just terrible! There was about ten or eleven people, that's children and all, and it was just a two-bedroom. They had a basement but that wasn't fit to live in. They didn't have no hot water because they had to shut it off because there was a gas leak, and that landlord wouldn't fix it. He told her she would have to move out if she couldn't fix it herself. That's when she came to us for help.

We got this Legal Aid attorney [to] come out and see her. This attorney got at the landlord and said, "You either fix that gas leak and that hot water, or else we'll turn you over to the city," and still he refused. This attorney turned him in to the city and he had to fix it, but after he fixed it, he raised her rent. She didn't want to rent there so she moved out here to Sioux Addition. She lives here now and that isn't any better than what she lived in before because she has to use a wood stove for heat. When it's cold, her house isn't that warm so her water freezes. So, she's still having problems.

If only we could get her away from her grandchildren, she could move into one of the high-rises. But you know, a lot of our elderly Indian people think they have to have all of their takozas with them, and in this case that's what's happening.

I'm also with that Pennington County Transportation group. We get a grant every year through the county and what we do is the ones that need to go to the doctor or to the meals programs, or shopping, we give them tickets and they use that to ride this transit bus. If you have your own money you can still ride those transit buses for eighty cents one way but a lot of our low-income elderly don't have that kind of money so you see a lot of them walking.

The average income for low-income is—a couple that gets ssi, they get something like $500-and-something a month. Now you know you can't live on that; especially if you have to pay your rent, your lights, your gas, your water, and you don't have that much to live on. A lot of them depend on their food stamps for a living but sometimes even that is not enough. So towards the end of the month you can go to Church Response; they give sacks of food to people that are needy. You have to go through all this red tape, "Do you get food stamps?" and "How long does it last you?" You know, I don't think it's right for them to be questioning a person about how they have to live, or what they do to make ends meet. If they didn't have to go begging for food they wouldn't be there! Church Response helps them maybe with a loaf of bread, a can of soup, a can of pork and beans, maybe a pound of meat. That cannot do much for a large family; maybe it could last a day or two and here they go hungry again.

Like in my case I get social security and that's from earnings from when I worked; it's about $632 but they take out some $30 for Medicare so I clear about $610 and that's what I live on. I'm living in a mortgaged home so I have to pay $62 a month, I have to pay for lights and gas, and this time of the year utilities are high because right now my gas bill is $300 for two months and my light bill is high because the heating operates by electricity. I pay for six things and by the time I get all that paid I usually have $300, maybe $200 and some dollars left in cash for my own use. So even that I can't live on because I have to have other things besides groceries and I don't get food stamps so I don't know how I manage.

I have a family of five children, three girls and two boys, but within the last three years, I lost two of my children. I lost a daughter named Mona Lisa in '87, and then my son passed away. He was forty-two years old. So I have three children left, two daughters and one son—my son lives here with me now. Then I keep a granddaughter that is the daughter of my daughter that passed away; she had three children.

Now, not bragging but my children are city bred. They went to school with white kids and they know that there's a lot of prejudice in Rapid City, but I tell them, "Don't let anybody push you around. You have the right to speak, this is America. I don't care if you're Indian, you have a voice. Don't be afraid to use it 'cause that's what I learned since I been here; I learned to stick up for my rights and that's what you kids have to do." I even tell the grandchildren that and they know it: "The minorities are mixed in with white society in this day and age. If you're going to go to school together, work together, you have to learn to be sociable, and try to have a better understanding so that you can fit into their social life." These are the things that we have to teach our generation now. Like they say, urban kids are too white orientated, so a lot of them don't know how to talk Indian, they don't understand Indian. They don't know the traditional but they're learning, you know. Nowadays, when we have a powwow, you'd be surprised how many of our little Indian kids are out there dancing, even blond-headed ones. [laughs] That's something they have to learn, so I think it's good that the parents teach them. They even have parents go to these schools to tell stories.

That reminds me—a year ago I was invited to the school. Little Joe, my grandson said, "Grandma, my teacher wants you to come over and tell some old Indian stories." So I did. [laughs]

I told them about Iktomi, that means "spider," you've heard about that. And I sang them this song about Mastincala [rabbit]. [sings] Mastincala nawizi na sinte onakislosloke. [Rabbit got jealous and kicked off his tail.]

I had to explain and I said, "You know this little rabbit got jealous of his companion, and he danced around and danced around till his tail flew off." [laughs] Oh, they got a kick out of it 'cause he was so jealous he lost his tail.

That Iktomi story is a good one! This Iktomi was moving down the trail, you know how Iktomis move, and here he come to a bunch of ants. He was looking at them and thinking, "Oh, they make good feed but I can't just go after them so I'll tell them a story." So he told them a story. He started telling them stories about how to survive and what the spiders do. Anyway, he sat there telling stories and pretty soon they went to sleep so he ate them up. [laughs]

That's similar to the prairie chickens, and what I want to do with this Indian story is in reference to what the government is doing to Mr.

Indian today, to all the Indian tribes. These prairie chickens get together and on a nice sunshiny day they're so happy they dance around; they flap their wings and close their eyes and dance all over and sing. One day, this coyote was sitting up there watching them on a hill and he saw them dancing and he says, "I wonder what they're dancing about? I'd like to get at them and have a good feed myself." So he sneaked up to them and he watched them dance, and pretty soon he was in there dancing with them. They saw him, they got scared and so he said, "Just keep dancing, I'll sing a song and you dance."—Of course if you tell it in Indian it's funnier.

Anyway, he said, "You're all pretty and you're doing a good dance. Just go ahead and keep flapping, close your eyes and dance." So he started singing them an Indian song and here they were all dancing and flapping their wings and closing their eyes.

So he sang for these prairie chickens and they danced and danced and he kept singing and singing, and pretty soon they dropped one by one. So he sang these prairie chickens to sleep. Then one prairie chicken noticed that he didn't hear wings flapping and so he opened his eyes and he said, "Run! Run everybody! That coyote is killing all of us!" and he took off because he finally woke up to the fact that the coyote had them all fooled, and this is what's happening with the government and the Indians today.

The old Indians, a few years back they were prairie chickens; they didn't pay attention to what the government was doing. They lived under the government and they were so used to hand-outs from the government this is what they were expecting, until the younger Indian people came alive. We have a lot of smart Indians nowadays that woke up to the fact that the government is just using them for this and that and taking their land away. Look at all the problems we're having with the Black Hills and trying to get them back and so the young Indian of today is fighting the government but it's too late; some of them say it's too late because the coyote done got them! [laughs] I really laughed when I heard this but that's my own interpretation of what's happening today.

There's an old song that everybody knows; it's called Inkpata. In the southern part of the valley there was two lovers. It was this man and this girl but they couldn't get along together, they couldn't communicate. So the man left her. So she stood up on the hill and she sang her love song to him, so he would come back. It goes something like this. [sings]

> *Inkpata nawajin na sina cicoze*
> [I was standing on a hill and waved my shawl]
> *Maya, maya, leci kuwa na.*
> [Oh my, oh my, come back over here.]

See, she was begging him to come back so she was waving her shawl, and waving it to come back to her, and that's what that's about.

Back in the olden days when the Indians were still wild, they used to have enemies; the other tribes were hunting one enemy down because they were trying to get the land. This group was camped along the river and they sent out their scouts to look around to see if there was any other tribes moving in on them. Before they send these two scouts out they told them, "You go prepared; pack all your gear, your bows and arrows and everything." So these two guys went out and they were scouting around. They didn't see nobody for miles around. Of course they usually go to the high places to scout and here they were so tired this one went to sleep. When he did wake up the other scout was gone and he listened to the ground and he could hear the enemy coming from somewhere but he didn't know where. He was thinking, "Well, maybe my friend is locating them and he'll come back and let me know." Pretty soon the sound got closer. They had long braids, these young scouts, so he took some of that smell-good Indian grease and started braiding his hair and greasing it all up and he had his moccasins off and his feet resting.

All of a sudden he heard a voice and he looked around and he heard it again and here it was his feet talking to him. They said to him, "Aren't you going to grease my soles? If you can't grease me, I won't run for you!" The foot was jealous of the braids 'cause he was greasing his braids, and so he looked at them and he said, "I will give you a good smell-good greasing if you'll promise to run away from the enemy and get me home safe." So after he greased the foot, he ran so fast that he got away from the enemy. He got home and warned the people that the enemy was coming and so that's the story of that one.

I told them different Indian fairy tales and about how precious the eagle is today. Then the teacher said, "Can you tell us about the medicine man, or something relating to that?" So I did tell them about all the different Indian herbs and things because I knew about my grandmother, so that came in handy! I always tell these kids, "In this day and age we don't have no medicine woman but in my day I had a grandma that was a medicine woman, and I had a grandpa that was a medicine man."

It's good to pass it on to the next generation.

Iola Columbus

IOLA COLUMBUS, *a Sisseton-Wahpeton Dakota, was raised on South Dakota's Flandreau Reservation. She lived more than forty years at Lower Sioux (Morton) Community, where in the 1970s she became the first woman in Minnesota to be elected tribal chair. As an elder, she traveled throughout the state developing a Grandmothers' Society that encouraged women elders to pass on their traditional knowledge to younger generations. She passed away on April 12, 1997, at age sixty-nine.*

I was born in Pipestone, Minnesota, but I was raised in South Dakota on a small reservation by my grandmother. I came from a real traditional background. I was raised in the traditional way, and by that I mean when I was about three or four years old my grandparents wanted to raise me. I imagine they told my mother, "Well, we choose this one to raise." The reason for that was to pass on their knowledge of our culture, the traditions and things, to one of the grandchildren. When I think of it, that's quite an honor. I didn't know it at the time, but that was the beginning of learning all our ways.

My grandfather didn't live too long after that, so it was just me and my grandmother that lived in Flandreau. Her name was Anna Wasu— translated, it's "Hail," that was her Indian name. It was really nice how we used to go and dig roots, and pick berries, and we'd pick tea and dry meat. I helped her tan hides, and we always put in a big garden too. All of these things were survival skills that she taught me. From the time of spring, first there was the tea that we picked, and then we dug turnips, and then we dug roots as they came into season for medicinal purposes. Then there was the time when we dried corn, and we dried meat. All of these things were by season.

We traveled a lot to go and see my parents. We went to Montana one time, and we camped way out in the hills someplace just to pick berries. Oh that was neat! We didn't have ice-boxes, they didn't have nothing like that then, so we had to eat wild game, ducks, and different kinds of animals. My brothers or elder members of the family would hunt those, and the women would clean them.

My grandmother used to say when we'd go dig medicines, "If there's two of them, take one, leave the other one so it can seed. Or if there's eight of them, you might be able to take five or six. You don't want to get greedy because that isn't good." There was a certain kind of medicine we used to go dig and she said, "This one woman got real greedy; she dug everything she seen in sight. Here, she was digging and digging that one time, and when she got to the end of this root there was a snake. So," she says, "Granddaughter, you don't want to get to that, where you're going to be greedy. Always be certain to give thanks. Take your tobacco or whatever, and always give thanks to the Creator because they're there for us to use."

One of my favorite times was in the winter because that was storytelling time. She'd tell me stories and she always said, "Come spring, I cannot talk about these things anymore." I used to wonder why but you just never questioned what your grandmother did.

Nowadays, when I give talks, they question a lot of that stuff and I said, "I can't answer some of these things because we just did what we were told to do, or we observed. I don't know what the reason is for that. I do know some of it but some of these things we cannot talk about, like ceremonial things. I can tell you how we did it but the outcome, or the purpose of it, some of these are very personal that we keep to ourself."

My grandmother talked to me about respecting and honoring people—young people, or old people, or little children, especially little children. I was taught by my grandmother that they were gifts from God, and that we needed to hold them, revere them, and that they were holy. "Even though they're babies, talk to them, they can't answer you but you are being heard."

She'd talk about having respect for other people, having respect for property, respect for everything. "These are God's creations" (of course she'd always say "Wakan Tanka" [Great Spirit]), "respect yourself."

She also used to say, "Granddaughter, when people come to see you, no matter if you just have tea or coffee, share that with them. One of the most important things is to share your food with people, and to share yourself. People are going to come to you, maybe when they're sad. People are going to come to you to share some good things that have happened. Share your time with them." That's our value system, sharing your time and yourself with other people.

I watched and I listened a lot to her teachings of being humble. There were times when I was in certain positions, I was kind of proud, and sometimes I wanted to show people that I had this authority, but I always remember what my grandmother said, not to put yourself above other people. Especially amongst our people; we are all relatives, and we honor and respect one another. So that helped me maintain the humility part of me.

They say that there's two things that an Indian person should have: the ability to laugh, the humor, and the ability to share. You get a lot of people like me who like to joke and you've got a circus; that's when you've got a lot of Indian people together socializing. They tell crazy jokes, or tease each other.

Teasing is a big part of our culture; there's certain ones can do that, certain ones can't. In-laws are very much respected. I never talked to my father-in-law, ever, not because I didn't like him but that's part of our culture. I always remember, we lived across the road here, and my father-in-law said to my husband, and I was standing right next to him, "Will you tell your wife to come over and make some bread for me?" He looked right at his son. They don't talk directly to their daughter-in-law and the same with the mother-in-law; they don't talk directly to their son-in-law, out of respect.

I didn't realize until after I grew up how important it was and how wonderful it was to have a grandmother, and having been raised that way it's helped me to survive some of the difficulties that have come to me.

I went to boarding school in Pipestone, Minnesota. I don't know the year but I must have been seven years old. It's funny how that happened because we were in Montana at the time, my grandmother and I, visiting my parents. We were going to stay with my parents that year. My dad was educated; he went to Lawrence, Kansas, that school there, and he worked as an engineer on roads. Anyway, they were in Montana, and my first year of school I went to public school at Wolf Point, Montana. After school, the white kids used to wait for us, and they used to stone us Indian kids.

I told my mother that, and my grandmother, so then in mid-term of my first year of school, they put me in a boarding school in Poplar, Montana. Still, we had to go to a white school but we boarded at an Indian-run dormitory-type school nearby. I went there and completed that year.

The first time I went to a government school, I didn't know I was going, and I didn't realize it until I got there. The only thing I can remember is that we were boarded on the school bus, and we traveled for about two or three days before we reached our destination, which was the Pipestone Indian School. I'm still trying to figure out why I was sent there, and the only logical reason I can think of is that I wasn't being treated right at the other schools. For that reason, perhaps, my parents, as well as my grandmother, decided that I needed to go to another school; they felt I should probably be in a safe place.

I don't have very pleasant memories of the school. All our matrons and teachers talked to us very harshly, and we were punished if we didn't do things right. They stressed cleanliness of course; that's the first thing they did in the morning. We had to line up. I was one of the little ones in first or second grade. The flooring was boards; we had to put our feet even with that line and the matron went down each row to see that we were all standing still. They checked to see if we washed our faces, combed our hair, and we had to hold our hands out and show that our nails were clean, and if they weren't, then they'd take a ruler and slap our hand.

If you didn't comb your hair, then one of the matrons would pull your braids, or slap you on your hand. My poor sister! I had long hair. I didn't want my hair cut, and so she used to have to get up extra early to comb my hair. The only kind of combs we had were tin combs, and it would pull your hair. So that was kind of a torture too but she did manage to comb my hair, and I didn't get my hair cut. [laughs]

They had one big room with all kinds of showers. Some of us were bashful and modest, yet there's nothing to cover you. It was really traumatic for some of us because we come from places where we didn't have that stuff.

It was like a military school. We were marched to and from wherever we were going, whether it was the dining hall, to the laundry room, to school, every place we went, we marched. It reminded me of herding a bunch of cattle.

On Saturdays and Sundays, we were allowed to go to town, and of course they chaperoned us every place. We had to wear woolen dresses, even during the summer, and itch, oh that was terrible! These long-sleeved woolen dresses; we wore them to town and to church, and they were dark red or dark green. So everybody knew where we were from, no matter where they seen us. "They're from that Indian school."

We were told not to speak the language. Even my grandmother and mother encouraged this. "You're going to go to school, you're going to work for white people. You might as well learn their language." So, I didn't teach my children, although my husband and I, when we don't want the kids to know something, then we speak our language. [laughs] They understand a little, they don't speak it. That's the sad part of it; I wished I would have taught them our language now.

When I lived with my grandmother, everything that we ate was fresh. In the winter time we cooked on a stove, but in the summer we did all of our cooking outside. So when I went to the government school, some of these foods were foreign to me. As a matter of fact it all was!

One of the ones that most of them didn't like was spinach. They had a dining-room matron; she walked around and made sure we ate our foods. It was terrible because some of those things we didn't care for, and some of them didn't hold it down 'cause they didn't like it.

That was the first time I ever seen a movie. We all assembled at the auditorium and they showed silent movies. I liked that, and I guess one other thing I have always liked is art. It gave us a chance to express our ideas of things. I think that was my favorite subject when I was in school there. Other than that, I really wasn't happy there.

In the meantime, my grandmother came back to Flandreau, South

Dakota, and that's only 18 miles from Pipestone. I wasn't there quite a whole year because when she came to see me, I was so lonesome and homesick, and I told my grandmother, "They're mean." To this day I wonder how she ever communicated; maybe she found somebody to interpret for her because she couldn't speak English, and yet she went somewhere and came back, and she says, "Ihun [That's not right!], I'm going to take you home." So, I must have had a tough little grandma because she took me home. [laughs]

Those are my memories of going to a boarding school. Nobody ever spoke to us kindly. It was always, "Do this!" In talking to a lot of Indian people over the years, something they resented very much was an authoritarian figure, especially if they spoke in a certain tone of voice. That stays in my mind very strong to this day. When people talk to me in a strict, firm voice, I won't be that cooperative. I know that about myself, which probably isn't too good.

When I was working at the shelter [for battered women] and they had workshops about being assertive, they always said that as Indians we were passive people. I used that as a lesson to my co-workers at the shelter. Some of the residents said that we had weren't very cooperative with some of the advocates, the non-Indians, because they came off in a certain way. So I used to try and tell my co-workers how to communicate with some of the residents. I said, "You're telling them, 'This, and this, and this are your options.' If you would take the time, especially listen, and then talk, it shows them that you care about them." I couldn't see being like that, so I did things different. As an Indian person, I practiced the way I talk to people and they appreciated that.

I could have been very defiant, you know, could probably have been a good activist. In the days when I was within the tribal government, I sort of told people just how I felt things should be, but before I did that, I always did my homework first to see that what I'm going to say was right. Then people believe you, and they support you in these issues, rather than just assuming that this is the way it's going to be. So those are the things I learned growing up and attending the school. In my opinion, some of the things that were negative somehow strengthened me to be how I am now.

So then I went to the public school at Flandreau for several years. They only had students from one to eighth grade, and then from Flandreau it was high school, from ninth to twelfth. I didn't complete my high school education but it wasn't because I didn't like it. My mother worked at a sewing factory, and she didn't earn very much. I didn't have the clothes and things that other girls had, so I chose to quit school.

The first time in my life I ever went to a big city, it was Sioux Falls. My girlfriend and I got a job there, and we were able to earn money and buy clothes. We worked in a laundry. I used to run that big ironing press. [laughs] We had it hard because we had to walk two miles to work every day. We didn't know the bus system, and we didn't have the money to ride the bus. We stayed at the Y. W. [Young Women's Christian Association]; we got a room there. We didn't have money for lunch, so we'd buy a loaf of bread and use something in between, not meat, maybe butter, or whatever. It was nice to get our first paycheck. We paid little rent at the Y. W., and we went out and ate a real good meal. [laughs]

I didn't think of us being poor, my grandmother and I, 'cause we always had something to eat but there were things that I knew that she would like. So, when I got my first check, after paying rent and buying groceries, we went back to Flandreau, South Dakota, and I gave my mother and grandmother each some money. I did that every now and then, always shared 'cause I knew that they went without things.

I used to always have this dream when I was young, "I'd like to live nice." I had been in a few homes of non-Indians, where they had a couch, where they had flowers, and things. I used to think "Some day I'm gonna live like that." When I lived with my grandmother, we had a table, we had a bed, the stove, a washstand—just the necessity stuff, nothing fancy—a few chairs, and we had mattresses, and we had feather ticks. I think everybody had them in them days.

We had two rooms. We had an upstairs but it wasn't finished, so when my mother and brothers came, all we'd do is throw down these feather ticks, and blankets, and then they have a bed. So after I seen these homes, I knew that there was other lifestyles. So I think that that was kind of my wish: someday to have a home.

At the time I didn't know it but when I look back, I didn't have a normal child life because I didn't have little kids to play with. I was around old people all the time. When we went to visit, my grandmother and I, we would go visit other older women. As I got older, I would do their dishes, sweep the floors for them. They would tell me how nice I was and they'd give me things. Somehow, I missed out playing with kids my age, and probably was lonely in a way, although I didn't think so at the time 'cause I had my grandmother. She was my whole life. Now, I watch my grandchildren, I see how they play and laugh. I didn't have that.

My grandmother taught me how to sew. I made my first quilt and completed it and entered in into a fair. They had what they call an "All-Indian Fair," where people brought their vegetables, brought their arts and crafts, and the judges gave you prizes: first, second, third. I won first prize on my quilt that I made for my age group. I also took vegetables from our garden and I got first prize on that. On the last day, they had a celebration; they didn't have no powwow or anything like that, they had a white[-style] dance.

They had a band come in, and I always remember it sounded so good, and people seemed to be enjoying themselves. I wanted to stay but it was starting to get dark and my grandmother wanted to go home. I liked what I seen, I liked the music I heard, and yet my grandmother said, "It's time to go home." I had no choice but to go home. I had to respect my grandmother but I was angry when I was going home, "If only I could stay and be with the other people."

So when I was alone and working, my girlfriend and I, we did those things that I missed out on. We met other Dakota girls, and we got acquainted with boys, and dancing. I liked socializing. Of course, sometimes it was rough; you get in with the wrong crowd. So that's the reason for me wanting to work, to have a different life than what I had. I think wanting to have a home so bad is one reason why I got married so young.

My sister was married and living in St. Paul and she was going to have her first child. They wanted somebody to baby-sit, so I said I would. I was kind of scared because it was a big city. She sent me my bus fare and I went on the bus to St. Paul. Nobody was there to meet me. So I gave the cab driver the address and he took me there. They weren't home. I got so scared I started crying. I just stood there till they came back, and I don't think I hardly ever left that building for a long time. Then they started taking me out after she had the baby. We'd go to dances and I used to love to dance. They were fox-trots, you know, and polka dances.

I was nineteen, or twenty, and it was there, at one of these places, that I met my husband, and that's the beginning of my life with a husband. [laughs] He really loves to dance. He'd get real fancy with me, and I'd get embarrassed because I couldn't dance that well. [laughs] So that was our way of entertainment throughout all these years, we'd go to different places and dance.

I got married when I was going on twenty-one. My husband had a family before; his wife died and he had a family. When I met him, he was so kind and he was witty; he made people laugh. I think I liked that about him. I told this to one person, "I don't know what love is, I really don't," I said, "but I think I married my husband because he made me laugh."

My grandmother always said that she was a "one-man woman." In her times, they had arranged marriages where your mate was picked for you. My grandmother, and my mother, both went through that. Their husbands were picked for them by their parents. She used to tell me, "Once you get married, you stay with that man, that's your mate for life." So, when my husband and I got married, I just made up my mind, "He will be my mate for the rest of my life, and through thickness, through thin, through sickness, through death." All of this I respected. I still do.

It's funny how you're raised has a lot to do with some of the decisions you make. My grandmother, although she lived the traditional way, respected our value system. She was a strict Episcopalian, so I was a confirmed Episcopalian too. She always said, "You need to be blessed, get married through the church."

Not knowing anybody in the city, so naive about everything, I went to the telephone book and under "churches" I was looking for "Episcopal." I called him [the minister], and I told him we would like to get married. So we set the date, and we got married in my husband's cousin's place. I later found out that he was next to the Bishop of Minnesota. [laughs] About twenty years afterwards, he came to our church here to ordain a priest and he said, "I married a couple from here," and he mentioned our names. I had the nerve to ask him! I didn't know who he was. He could have been the pope for all I know. [laughs]

I got married in 1948. I moved here and have lived here ever since, so that's forty-three years I've lived in this place, at Lower Sioux Community.

Moving from South Dakota, from the kind of background and the traditions I was used to, when I moved into my husband's community, it was like a culture shock. By that I mean these people were already adapted to the white people's ways. I was uncomfortable even in meeting with the other Indian women. They had Women's Guild but it was strange for me. Even to this day there's a difference. I think that I belong here but I feel different amongst the people because they didn't keep up their traditions and that's really what I miss.

When I go out west, we go to powwows and different ceremonies—when I speak of "west" I mean Pine Ridge and Rosebud, Cheyenne River, these different places—I feel so at ease because these people have maintained their traditions. I could see that, I watched them, how their children run around, and the grandmothers are so protective of their kids, and how the people honor the elderly. Here where white society is dominant you could see the difference.

These are families that moved back after the war [1862 Dakota Conflict]. They live in what you call "old assignments"; they call it "1862 land," which means they started this reservation. After the 1934 Indian Reorganization Act was passed, then this reservation became known as an "Indian Reorganization Reservation," and along with it came all these laws.

We had an agent, through the government, who would periodically come over here just to see what the people were doing. He noticed they were doing some of these ceremonial things and he said, "You cannot practice your Indian traditions because that's paganism." So then they quit doing these things; in some ways they'd sort of sneak it but after a while, then Christianity took over.

So to this day Christianity has had a big impact on the people here and they've almost lost their spiritual Indian ways. But slowly, the young people are beginning to recognize that we did have a beautiful culture and we'd like to go back to that but they don't have the old people to teach them our values or the traditional ways. So then what's happening is that they go to different reservations; we have some men here who have a mentor who tells them that "this is the way it used to be done." So they're trying to bring that back.

I had ten children—I have nine living, we lost one son. When I was younger, I used to be like a mother bear. In some ways I'm still like that. I hear people say, "If I had to do things over, I wouldn't have so many kids because that's the reason why I'm poor," or "I would have did things different." I'd sit there thinking, "I couldn't do that because this child is very special and each one has their little niche." My family means a lot to me, so I would say that that's kind of been my career. My children are my life and I don't know if I'd ever want to change it.

I was so busy raising kids there for a while. Every now and then we'd go to powwows, but I didn't dance. We did pick it up later on because some of my children had an interest, especially my youngest daughter. I made her outfits, and I'm trying to do the same with my grandchildren. I still like to dance every now and then at powwows. I get out there and it's just good to be amongst your own people; you hear your own language, and you eat ethnic foods. It's such a good feeling you forget about your aches and pains.

My mother always managed to spend time with my children and they all really loved their grandmother. I used to watch her, and I kind of envied my mother in some ways; she could get my children to do things that I couldn't get them to do. Sometimes, in order to get them to do something, I used to raise my voice and come off the way they treated us in the government school. But my mother had a certain way with them. She joked, and she teased them.

There was a period in my life where my children drank alcohol and were involved in other things that I didn't approve of and felt that I didn't have control over. I used to think, "I must be a rotten parent. My children are doing all of these terrible things," and just blame myself. I used to think, "I didn't teach them anything." Now, they've been through treatment, they've been to different counseling, their lifestyle is changing. I see what they're doing now.

My sons are all hunters, they're all outdoorsmen, they like fishing. What I'm really proud of is that when they get a deer, they'll share it with the elderly or with people who can't get that otherwise. My sons give thanks for that animal that they got because we are to use it for food and nothing else. My sons will help people who are in need, like shoveling somebody's driveway, or doing jobs that somebody else won't do. So when I see them helping people like that, I think, "Well, maybe they did learn something."

My daughters too, they're very helpful; they'll help a woman who maybe has little children, who's sickly. My daughter bakes at Christmas time or special days and shares her baking with people. These are things that I like to see in my children, where they're sharing their time, and also food and things. So maybe something that I told them did kind of sink in.

Here you love your children, but those little grandchildren—they look at you with their little eyes. It just sort of melts you; they can make you do anything. [laughs] Still, I know you have to teach them too. I try to spend as much time with them as I can. I think I have twenty-four. When I do come home after being gone for a week, then they come all at once. Sometimes that gets to be overwhelming. [laughs]

I wish I could take them out in the woods, or in the meadows. Here, we're such a small community, there isn't much land. Where there's meadows and pasture lands, we can't get at it because there's "No Trespassing" signs. You can't just go take a walk in a field or a meadow, and pick flowers and look for roots and stuff. That's impossible these days.

I do beadwork when I have time. I made ribbon shirts, and then I'd bead little novelty things but that was to pass time away. If I was to do that for a living, I wouldn't make much money. [laughs] I do love to read but I don't find time for that either anymore. I'm busy trying to help my children.

Living in a community where there's tribal politics, you find that you feel that your children aren't being treated equal. If I'm not satisfied with something that's going on, I do the background work on it before I approach the council. That way I know what I'm talking about. You need to know the laws if you're going to deal with some of the leaders. So I find myself helping my children in ways like that because I, myself, have been in tribal politics. I was on the council for ten years.

This was back in the early seventies, or maybe even '69. There were no jobs around here, so the men had to go away from this area to work. Some of them went to Minneapolis, some of them went to canning factories in Fairmont. There were mostly women here; the men were gone for the week and then they'd come back.

We had a tribal government, but there was no funds on which to operate any programs. So when election time came around, somebody had put in my name, and I didn't decline. I was curious; what do they do? One way to find out is to get in there. So I was nominated and when election came around I was voted in as the secretary-treasurer.

I don't know if I should say this but maybe this would shed some light on what I'm gonna say later on. At this one meeting, some important issue came in and usually the full council, which is five members, have to be there in order for anything to pass. I was sick and I wasn't able to come. One of the council members made this remark, "We really don't need Iola, she's dumb." I heard that back and it stuck with me for a long, long time. And the reason why I was treated like that was I was a non-member, yet I was able to serve on the council. "She's from another reservation, we are from here." I heard that through all these years; even up to this day they'll say, "Well, she's a Sisseton-Wahpeton."

So I kept that in mind but I was learning for that year; I just learned the functions of this council, the tribal government, and the authority that they have. I had my input but I didn't do too much. Time went on where I became a tribal chairperson.

We didn't even have a meeting hall. So I did some investigating, doing some contacting on my own, to see if there were funds available to get a tribal center where we could put all our documents, where we could have our meetings, where we could have meals. I got some funds through the Bureau, and also through HUD.

One of the stipulations was that we have a place for the seniors. By then we were pretty well established as an active council. We had four women on the council and one man, and he didn't like that too well. We started getting in more and more funds for housing, we started getting more funds for Indian Health, and social services.

Once there was funds, and once there was some authority attached to it, then the men became interested. Then there were jobs available because we had funds to operate these programs, so then they became interested in these positions.

Then back in '78 or '79 I retired and announced to the community that I no longer wanted to be in that role, that I would seek something else. But because I was the first one to do that, I acquired a lot of enemies. They said I was forcing these laws onto the people.

Anytime there was funds for housing, I went by the needs. We had to make decisions. They didn't see it that way. They said since I'm the head person, "She's favoring that one." So that's why I felt being involved in politics created a lot of mistrust and I didn't want to be in that. So they're seeing me in a different light now.

I don't know that they noticed if I was getting older or not. What kind of bothered me was that people would come to me and present tobacco to me. They'd come and ask me certain things and I was thinking, "Do I have the right? Am I worthy or what? I'm not a medicine woman." But somehow or another, they recognized that I was there, I was that person, and it bothered me so much that I talked to some other elder women and also to a medicine man. "Am I doing the right thing? Is it proper for me to do these things?"

They said, "When you reach a certain stage in your life, when you become an elder, you have all those rights. You have the right to talk to people, you have the right to talk to men, you've earned that now." Before women always stood in the background, and men were our spokesperson. Now we have that right to voice our opinion and let people know how things should be.

So I think the people somehow know when you're going through that stage. I have reached the ranks of an elder, and they recognize that. And yet when I'm with a group of elders, I mean elderly elders, I'm thinking about eighty, ninety years old, it makes me feel so humble that here are people who have a wealth of wisdom. I'm just like a baby elder. [laughs] I don't know what else to call it but I'm just beginning! [laughs]

In some ways I don't even think of myself as an elder because I'm able to get around, I'm able to help other people; so it makes me forget that I'm in that range. I have to remind myself, even sometimes the way I dress. I buy clothes that are kind of youthful. [laughs] "Gee whiz, what would my grandmother think if she seen me dress like this?" My grandmother wore nothing but dresses. She wore black stockings and little scarves, and all those things that are characteristic of an American Indian grandmother.

The Indian people used to have certain rites for different periods in their life, an infant, and then a youth, and then reaching manhood, and then after that pretty soon you're a father, and then after that you go into elder. So there's different ways that they respected, or honored, different stages of your life.

I talked to a group of college students and there was two men in there. They were very quiet. You know how the women are; after I gave my presentation they had a lot of questions. One of them said, "Iola, where are the men at today? What is their role?" When I give my talks, I feel that in order for them to completely understand what I'm trying to put across, you always have to have a story with that. So I used as an example, what happened with my son and my grandmother.

I used to want my children to know their great-grandmother, my grandmother. We lived here, and my oldest son must have been about nine, ten years old. He wanted to take Kunksi [Grandmother] something. So he went fishing early in the morning. He must have brought about six little bullheads. "I'll bring this to her," he said.

I thought, "These are too small," but I know my grandmother; she would eat them anyway. It was in July, and hot—eighty-some degrees. I thought, "I'll put them in some water and maybe they'll keep till we get there." We used to take it slow because we had an older car. I cleaned them, and we put them in the car and away we went. That's a hundred-some miles from here.

When we got there to my grandmother's place, my son jumped out of the car, took his little pail, and he gave that to my grandmother. She was so thankful, "Oh Takoza [grandchild], thank you, thank you. Had this been back in the old days, grandson, I would have been required to eat one of them raw. You have reached manhood now because you're able to hunt and fish." They were all right, she cooked them and ate them and my son was so proud, because in his grandmother's eyes he was recognized as a man, and he was able to do something to prove it.

So I think that's what it's like these days. We raise our children and sure, they go to school, but nobody recognizes them for what they've done or when they've reached that, so some of them continue being a young person all their life.

I ended up telling these two men, I said, "What I think has happened with our men, some of that has phased out and we no longer recognize a man as a provider, as a protector. That's gone." I said a few other words just to encourage them to try to understand things. But that got them to talk, and that got them to smile, when I told them that. Otherwise, they were just sitting there and all these women; you know how we are! [laughs]

You have different phases, like when a boy reaches manhood you can honor him, have a ceremony for him. I had one of my sons honored way in Pine Ridge one year because they don't do that here. But slowly now because of the powwows here every year, people are beginning to know and learn that we need to honor this for that; we need to give thanks for this and that.

We honor our little ones at different times of their life. At the powwow, we had my two grandsons honored because they were coming out for the first time dancing in full regalia. We had a little giveaway because people seen them dance for the first time, so we as grandparents did that.

One of the more frequent ceremonies is they honor a man who's in the service, who has either joined the military service, or has come back from war, then they're honored at the powwows. What's really neat is if he has an Indian name—say for instance, his name is Spotted Eagle— the drummers will make a song with his name and whatever else the family wants.

They'll say, "He went away to war, he was wounded there, or else he did something spectacular, some brave thing." They'll mention that in that song. They'll have a "eyapaha"—it means "master of ceremonies"—announce all of this and he'll explain what's going to take place.

They'll have him [the person being honored], along with the family, dance, go in a circle. The people who are honoring him, the supporters, will all go and shake hands with him and that family. After they complete that song, then the family might have a giveaway. That's their way of expressing their appreciation for what's taken place. They'll feed after they get through with this giveaway, and they also give something to the people who made the song for their loved one.

Another one is birthdays. They'll honor a person whose birthday is that day, or maybe somebody graduated from high school. You can be honored for everything—it's as a person wishes. They do that because they love that person and they want people to know, "We love them so much."

We need to give thanks, offer thanks. I used to think giving thanks [meant saying] "Thank you," for someone who does something for you, but in our Indian way it goes further than that. It isn't so much thanking a person, it's thanking Wakan Tanka for everything and you'll be blessed for that. These are all parts of our value system.

I think we need to reactivate our role as a grandmother and we don't have to be afraid because these things are allowable. The federal government passed different laws that didn't allow us to do certain things but now we can practice some of our ways through the Freedom of Religion Act.

When women are what we call "in their moon," we keep them isolated during that time. Really, that's nice too, because you don't have to do all the other things, your tasks; that would be your chance to rest. We don't do that anymore but they do at sundances.

Out in Dakota country they're saying that the men are telling their women that they need to dress as women. This is one of the requirements at a sundance. Did you know that? [laughs] I made the mistake of going to a sundance, I was in such a hurry I didn't put on a dress. So after we got into the arena—you have to take off your shoes and they give you sage—my husband and I were called to the center and they were going to honor us.

And one lady said, "Since you didn't wear a dress, take this shawl and wrap it around." Well, this shawl just barely covered me and it kept wanting to fall off. I was so embarrassed, I knew I should have put on a dress but in my hurry I didn't do that.

So that's what some of the men are saying, you know, "The women nowadays are trying to be more like a man; they even dress like a man; they cut their hair like a man; they want to get paid the same wages as a man. They want to be equal to a man." They don't like it. One person even went as far as to say that in our ceremonies, our spirits don't recognize the women as women because they look so much like men. "Oh dear," I said, "That's terrible!" [laughs]

I do have an Indian name; it's He Hota Win, or Gray Horn Woman, and there is a story about it. It's another part of our Indian traditions that I think is really important because the name is given to you for a purpose:

you are to be like that person. For instance, one of my grandmothers—I believe there was six or seven sisters—one of them had this name. According to the relatives, they said she was a humble person, yet she had leadership quality. The other sisters listened to whatever she said because she was very wise.

The story is, she and her sisters were walking across this meadow and a farmer had just cut down the hay. While she was walking, she was the one that was observing. She watched and seen everything, and here she found a skunk tail. It had been cut off by this farmer while he was cutting the hay. She took it home and she singed it, and she cooked it and ate it. Well, apparently this one grandmother loved meat, and she did like to cook and was particular about her meat. They said I possessed that quality which is true; I'm particular about my meat.

Before I got this name, all my relatives had to agree, "Is she that kind of person? Is she honest, is she this type?" I told my mother, "I don't know if I can be that person." I was really worried that maybe some of my relatives wouldn't agree that I could have that name. I don't know how long it was before, "Yes," they said, "We'll let her have that name. We think she possesses some of those qualities."

So even today, I think about that: "Am I doing right? Do I live up to that?" That name kind of molds you to what you are. And that's what I think is really neat about these name-giving ceremonies. These are thought over carefully, to see if you can be like that person. It helps you.

That isn't always the case. Some of them get their name at an early age. Back in the old days, like my grandmother's days, you earned that too. Also it was probably something spectacular that happened to you.

For instance, our family name, had the missionaries or somebody asked, would have been "His Day" instead of "Columbus" because my husband's grandfather's name was Anpektetawa. He didn't know what it was that his grandfather did to earn that name.

In his later years he [her husband] wanted an Indian name because one of the things we believe is that when you go into the spirit world, you're more accepted if you have an Indian name. Being his age—I forget how old he was—he wanted that, and the relatives said, "Sure." We had a medicine man come and we had the ceremony right here and he acquired that name, Anpektetawa. It had to do with something that happened on a certain day. We never did find the story out about that, because all the elderlies had gone on, but that was the name that he thought that he would have and they would recognize when he went into the spirit world.

So that's another one of our traditions which I think are very helpful. Some of my children have names, some of them don't. We still have to have it officially done, where we have the ceremony, the giveaway, the feast and everything. Then they can have the name for the rest of their lives. We had that done for some of my grandchildren, and we did it in a contemporary way. It was done by a medicine man but it was also done in a church so that it's down in the baptismal records.

I feel so strongly about preserving our Indians ways, our culture. That is why I'm trying to organize this Grandmothers' Society, and talking to the grandmothers, trying to encourage them to pass on their knowledge to the young people because a lot of them weren't raised that way.

It isn't so much that I think they should learn how to bead or these things. It would help them to know what an Indian turnip looks like, or what cherries look like, and how to preserve those things, but more important is our value system. I think that's why we've survived as a nation.

I try to meet with women who've been brought up in a traditional way and the ones that are knowledgeable about our values and culture. I encourage them to share that with other women because I feel that we have been silent for too long. I'm finding that there's a lot of things we can share to help our Indian women. The people that I've been talking with have been very supportive and want to be involved.

It cannot be a project, it has to be like a movement. Once you start it as an organization, you're going to need a leader; you need a chairman, you need a vice-chair, you need someone to take minutes; you need to have funds. You're setting up a hierarchy then, and we don't want that because we want all these grandmothers to be equal.

You can't say, "I want the grandmothers to join the society, and to be qualified you got to be a certain age and have this knowledge," because there are grandmothers that are young nowadays, and we can't discriminate. Each one of us might have one thing that you could share with the rest of us that is of value. She might have had a beautiful childhood and learned things from her grandmother that she could share. I'm hoping that by letting these women know that, they in turn will pass that on, and that it'll just keep going like that.

There's a lot that I don't know. The Ojibwe grandmothers, there's certain things that they do differently, and I want us to appreciate all of that, and to understand that. That's why I want to get that message across real clear, that we're just a group of grandmothers who are trying to let the people know, or encourage them, to go back to practicing our values. I believe that through that, our young people will begin to appreciate their identity. That's the purpose of this Grandmothers' Society.

Hopefully we'll end up talking about some of these things that we all share in common, but first we need to establish some trust. One of the things that I try to do is to encourage some of these women to talk about some of the most difficult times in their lives. Some of these grandmothers have top positions and are still working. They want a support group because they feel that when they have crises, and situations, they didn't have nobody to go to because they're considered to be the top.

Sometimes there's actually abuse. They're being abused by their relatives, they don't want to talk about it. It's a dishonor, disgrace, to talk about your husband, or whoever it is. That's why if they could talk to another woman and they can say, "This is what I do; this is what I did," this type of information they could share. And the women are anxious for it. One woman said, "Perhaps if we had such a group, I would have had you to talk to. I wouldn't have to go and share that with a total stranger."

There's no way that they can go to a younger person and share this information because everybody knows them to be an elder and we have all that wisdom. That's where I feel that the grandmothers can really be helpful in comforting one another and sharing this information.

That's what I would like it to become. Right now we're just mainly trying to be recognized as the Grandmothers' Society, and also how we can reach the other grandmothers and encourage them to share their skills and knowledge with the younger generation.

They had what you call Spiritual Unity of Tribes; it was held in New Mexico. It was really beautiful because what surprised me was that it was like we were all in the same brain wave. As I sat there and I listened to different ones that gave presentations, everything that I was thinking they said. I mentioned that when I gave my presentation because this gathering was to honor the grandmothers.

I gave them thanks and I said, "I think we're all here for a reason, it was made possible for us all to be here. No matter where I go, what I do, it's spirit-led." The non-Indians that were there came over to our camp when we were sitting there eating. They said, "We were told by our leaders that it's time to learn the ways of the Indian because they've survived all of this. We need to learn their ways." They came from all different denominations; there were Buddhists, Mormons, Bahais.

They want to learn our ways, and I couldn't help but tell about this medicine man I met with when I was wondering what my role was. I had a special ceremony and I left it up to the Great Spirit. The medicine man put it this way. "Iola", he said, "the Great Spirit made these races, the red, black, yellow and white. As a grandmother not only do you share your knowledge with just Indian people, you have to share it with the other races."

So I thought of that because I used to be kind of stingy about certain things. I didn't want them to know about us. Another thing that kept me from talking was most of the people that go out and give lectures have degrees, they're professors, or doctors of such-and-such. I had low self-esteem and I'd think, "I'm not educated and nobody's going to listen." All this kind of stuff I used to think but that kind of helped me after talking to the spiritual leader. The Great Spirit isn't looking at what degree you have; you have to share. That's why I made that commitment that I will do that. From day one, grandmothers were the teachers, counselors, protectors of a tribe. We need to continue that.

The reception has been real good. The Minnesota Historical Society asked me to give a talk at the Interpreters Center here [at Lower Sioux]. It just came up sudden like, you know I didn't have time to prepare what I was going to talk about. This other girl was supposed to demonstrate beading but she was very shy. They asked us to share a little about the history of this place. I thought, "Well, it's Sunday, there won't be too many people."

Sometimes I get sort of shy too, but there was a lot of people at the center. I began talking about this area, and about our role as women, how they learned to bead, and clothe the family, about some of the foods that the Indian people introduced to the non-Indians, corn and squash, and how men were the protectors of the women.

If you look at the animals, the birds, the males' feathers are brighter, where the women, they don't have too much color. A male pheasant is more colorful than the female, and that's to protect or distract the prey. In a joking way I said, "Maybe in this day and age we need to dress our men like that too so they can protect the women." Everybody just laughed and I didn't really mean to say it like that but it turned out that way, so it turned out real good. [laughs] Sometimes they're amazed that we can even talk the way we do!

So once I get these grandmothers organized in Minneapolis, where they know what they want to do, then I can go on to these other reservations and have a chapter there, till it's all over the state of Minnesota. I know all these tribal chairmen and I have a good rapport with them, so I feel that I can go on any of these reservations and say that I would like to give a presentation, and they'd approve of it.

Once we do that, I have personally made a commitment that what I'm doing is not only limited to Indian people. Like I said, the medicine man said, "Iola, you no longer share your information, or your skills and knowledge with just Indians. The Great Spirit, the Creator, created four races, red, yellow, white and black. You need to work with the people. They're all eager to know how it is the Indian people come to survive. There must be some way that we can teach other nations about our ways. We need to share that information with them." So, that's another part of my dream, you might say.

Acknowledgments

For their help in supporting my work
I would like to thank the following people:

Sara Remke for her all-important phone call.
Janet Spector for her encouragement during our
    serendipitous meeting at the co-op.
Susan Geiger for her glowing letters of recommendation.
Juanita Espinosa for her insight and wisdom.
Monika Bauerlein for her brilliance, creativity,
    and editorial guidance.
Jerome Kills Small for his assistance with the translations.
Pat Carlson for her friendship, loyalty, and humor.
Nigel Grigsby for his wit and friendship.
Jean Brookins, Ann Regan, Debbie Miller, and *Marilyn Ziebarth*
    at the Minnesota Historical Society for their patience,
    wit, and commitment.
Finally, I wish to thank my family, *Jane Penman, Alethea Barros,*
    and *Stephanie Barros* for their love and laughter.

Honor the Grandmothers was designed and set in type at the Minnesota Historical Society Press by Will Powers. The types are Minion, designed by Robert Slimbach in 1989, and Ex Ponto, designed by Jovica Veljovic in 1995. This book was printed by Thomson-Shore, Inc., in Dexter, Michigan.